THE NEW TEMPLE AND THE SECOND COMING

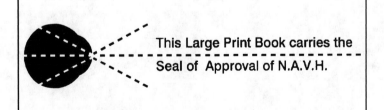

This Large Print Book carries the
Seal of Approval of N.A.V.H.

THE NEW TEMPLE AND THE SECOND COMING

THE PROPHECY THAT POINTS TO CHRIST'S RETURN IN YOUR GENERATION

GRANT R. JEFFREY

WALKER LARGE PRINT

An imprint of Thomson Gale, a part of The Thomson Corporation

Detroit • New York • San Francisco • New Haven, Conn. • Waterville, Maine • London

THOMSON

™

GALE

Walker Large Print Originals.

The text of this Large Print edition is unabridged.

Other aspects of the book may vary from the original edition.

Set in 16 pt. Plantin.

LIBRARY OF CONGRESS CATALOGING-IN-PUBLICATION DATA

Jeffrey, Grant R.
    The new temple and the Second Coming : the prophecy that points to Christ's return in your generation / by Grant R. Jeffrey.
        p. cm.
    Includes bibliographical references.
    ISBN-13: 978-1-59415-235-1 (lg. print : alk. paper)
    ISBN-10: 1-59415-235-7 (lg. print : alk. paper)
    1. Bible — Prophecies — Temple of Jerusalem. 2. Temple of Jerusalem (Jerusalem) 3. Second Advent. 4. Large type books. I. Title.
    BS649.J4J44 2008
    236'.9—dc22   2007043618

Published in 2008 by arrangement with WaterBrook Press, a division of Random House, Inc.

Printed in the United States of America on permanent paper
10 9 8 7 6 5 4 3 2 1

CONTENTS

PREFACE 7

Introduction: Rebuilding the Temple . 11
*The Countdown to Christ's
Return*

1. Preparing the Way for the
Third Temple 25
*Recent Discoveries Have
Removed Several Major
Obstacles to Rebuilding*

2. The Glory of Jerusalem's Temple . . 47
*Re-creating the Sanctuary of
God on Earth*

3. Recovering Lost Temple Treasures . 69
*Pursuing the Clues Found in
the Copper Scroll*

4. Exploring the Ancient City
Underneath Jerusalem 91
*Fascinating Discoveries in the
Subterranean City*

5

5. The Third Temple in the
    Last Days 123
    *How Plans to Build the
    Temple Signal Christ's Soon
    Return*
6. Practical Preparations for
    Rebuilding the Temple 149
    *Reconvening the Sanhedrin,
    Recovering the Oil of
    Anointing, and Preparing for
    the Red-Heifer Sacrifice*
7. New Vessels for Temple Worship . . 175
    *Re-creating the Sacred
    Instruments Used in Old
    Testament Sacrifice*
8. The Ark of the Covenant and
    the Third Temple. 203
    *Reliable Reports on the
    Location of the Ark*
9. Preparing for the Coming
    Messiah 233
    *The Events of the Last Days
    Are Upon Us*

    APPENDIX: POSSIBLE SEQUENCE
        OF KEY PROPHETIC EVENTS . 263
    NOTES. 269
    SELECT BIBLIOGRAPHY 281

PREFACE

The New Temple and the Second Coming is the result of more than four decades of detailed research into the history, archaeology, and prophetic future of the Temple in Jerusalem. A lifetime of intense study of the Scriptures, plus reading hundreds of books and interviewing dozens of archaeologists, historians, and respected rabbis, all have provided me with valuable insights into the Temples of God that have stood on the Temple Mount. Over the last two decades my wife, Kaye, and I have had the privilege of exploring numerous tunnels, cisterns, and caverns beneath the Holy City, enabling me to understand some of the many mysteries of Jerusalem and the Temple's history.

As this book will demonstrate, we are witnessing the fulfillment of numerous prophecies regarding the rebuilding of the Temple in our generation. The practical preparations to build the Third Temple are the clearest signs yet that we are rapidly approaching the time when the Messiah will return to set up His holy kingdom on earth. We are living in the generation that will witness the Second Coming.

Jesus Christ encouraged believers not to fear but rather to be filled with hope when we see the fulfillment of these unique prophecies. Christ declared: "And when these things begin to come to pass, then look up, and lift up your heads; for your redemption draweth nigh" (Luke 21:28).

My late father and my mother inspired me by their deep commitment to Christ and their lifelong interest in the prophecies of His Second Coming.

I dedicate this book to my loving wife, Kaye. She continues to inspire my research and writing as well as being my faithful partner in our research, explorations, and writing ministry. Without her encouragement and constant assistance, this book would never have been completed.

I trust that my research will inform, inspire, and encourage you to personally study the Bible's prophecies about the remarkable prophetic events that are setting the stage for the return of Christ.

Grant R. Jeffrey
Toronto, Ontario
June 2007

Introduction:
Rebuilding the
Temple
THE COUNTDOWN TO CHRIST'S RETURN

■ ■ ■ ■

Watchman, what of the night?
Watchman, what of the night?
The watchman said, The morning cometh,
and also the night:
if ye will enquire, enquire ye:
return, come.

Isaiah 21:11–12

Almost two thousand years ago, after nearly two years of terrible siege, the brutally efficient legions of Rome destroyed Jerusalem and burned the Temple to the ground. Led by General Titus, the son of Emperor Vespasian, the Roman army completed its mission of destruction on the ninth day of Av (August) in AD 70.

The glorious Temple, built by King Herod, was the second of the sacred Temples to stand on the Temple Mount in Jerusalem. The First Temple had been built by King Solomon around 1000 BC and was destroyed by the Babylonians in 586 BC. The Second Temple, built initially by the Jews after their return to Jerusalem in 536 BC following the Babylonian captivity and then expanded by Herod in the first century, remains in ruins today. However, exciting developments are taking place in Israel that will result in a Third Temple being built on the ancient foundations that Solomon put in place more than three thousand years ago. You and I are part of the generation that will live to see a Temple of God once again stand in Jerusalem, the spiritual crossroads of the world.

The rebuilding of the Temple holds profound prophetic significance, equal to the appearance of the Antichrist or the forming of the pagan armies to invade Israel in the coming War of Gog and Magog. While many students of biblical prophecy have debated the role that will be played by the Third Temple in end-times developments, the Scriptures make it clear that just before Christ returns, the Third Temple of God must stand again on the original location on the Temple Mount.

Preparations to rebuild the Temple have progressed on several fronts, with plans already in place that go into far greater detail than most people are aware of. The Temple project is yet another major prophetic signpost on the time line leading to the final conflict of the battle of Armageddon and the establishment of the kingdom of God. No less a prophet than Jesus Christ made it clear that the generation that witnessed the return of the Jews to the Promised Land would live to see Him return to earth. The modern State of Israel was born in 1948, which means that you and I are part of the last-days generation (see Matthew 24:32–34). However, the Temple must once again occupy its place on the Temple Mount before the major prophesied events of the last days can take place.

Many scholars have questioned whether the Temple will ever be rebuilt because of the immense practical, religious, and political obstacles that stand in the way. Mosques, shrines, and other Muslim holy sites occupy the Temple Mount, a thirty-five acre site that is under the administrative control of Arab authorities. Since the Six-Day War in 1967, Israel has controlled the entire city of Jerusalem, including the Temple Mount. However, Israel allows the Supreme Muslim Religious Council (the Waqf) to control religious activities and to police (without firearms) all activities on the Temple Mount. This area is the location of the Dome of the Rock and the Al-Aqsa Mosque. Religious Jews do not worship in the area of the Dome of the Rock because the chief rabbis warn they might inadvertently trespass on the site of the ancient Holy of Holies. Muslim control of the Temple Mount fulfills the prophecy of Luke 21:24, that "Jerusalem shall be trodden down of the Gentiles, until the times of the Gentiles be fulfilled."

In addition to the political and religious tensions that stand in the way of rebuilding the Temple, a longstanding and seemingly unsolvable dilemma from within Judaism has presented a major obstacle. The Jews cannot rebuild the Temple or resume worship in the Temple unless the long-dormant Sanhedrin Court, the highest body of Jewish lawmakers, is reconvened. This is necessary in order to reestablish the Levitical priesthood. The Sanhedrin is the only religious body authorized to determine the correct location of the Temple, to reinstitute the ancient rituals, and to oversee the many details related to Temple ritual and worship.

One of Jesus' prophecies indicates that the Sanhedrin will indeed be fulfilling its duties in the last days. Christ warned His disciples about the coming persecution in Jerusalem during the Tribulation. He told them to pray that their flight from the city would not be "on the sabbath day" (Matthew 24:20). The reason for this is the commandment against performing work on the sabbath (see Exodus 20:8–10). The ancient Sanhedrin had determined that any travel on the sabbath that exceeded one thousand paces was considered work. However, if an invasion force should attack on the sabbath and the Jews in Jerusalem limited their travel to one thousand paces, it would ensure their destruction. Christ's prophecy implies that the Sanhedrin will exist in the last days and will have the authority to enforce such a religious rule. The historian Flavius Josephus calculated the distance from the Temple Mount to the Mount of Olives, known popularly as "the sabbath's day journey," as approximately one thousand yards.[1] Interestingly, the gospel historian Luke wrote in the book of Acts that the distance from the Mount of Olives to the Temple Mount is approximately a thousand paces, a "sabbath's day journey" (1:12).

ISRAEL WITHOUT A TEMPLE

With the destruction of the Second Temple in AD 70, Israel lost the Temple as the center of its spiritual life (see photograph). During the nineteen centuries that followed, Jews in exile prayed for their prophesied return to the Promised Land. Every year at Passover and at the end of Yom Kippur, righteous Jews have prayed, "Next year in Jerusalem." Along with that hope, religious Jews have longed to rebuild their Temple and establish the long-promised kingdom of

God on earth under the rule of the long-awaited Messiah.

Over those same centuries, three times a day devout Jews living in exile have prayed that they will live to see their Temple rebuilt: "May it be Thy will that the Temple be speedily rebuilt in our days."[2] They looked forward to the day when the Temple would once again stand on the Temple Mount. They longed for the Lord to return His Shekinah Glory and Divine Presence to the sanctuary in Jerusalem.

Finally, after nineteen centuries, today's generation has been given the task of making these ancient dreams come true.

This scale model is an accurate representation of the Second Temple, which was destroyed by the Roman legions in AD 70.

18

God's Command to Build a Sanctuary

The rebuilding of the Temple is central to the messianic hopes of the Jewish people. As the rabbis have noted, God never rescinded His command that Israel build a sanctuary for Him (see Exodus 25:8). Therefore, His command remains in force today.

The Lord gave Moses the precise blueprint to follow in constructing His earthly sanctuary, the movable Tabernacle that Israel used prior to the building of the First Temple. The sacred vessels and worship instruments that later were used in Solomon's Temple, including the ark of the covenant, were modeled by Moses' craftsmen according to the pattern of the sacred objects in the eternal Temple in heaven (see Exodus 25:8–9; Hebrews 8:5). Likewise, God revealed to King David and his son Solomon the detailed plans for building a permanent Temple on Mount Moriah in Jerusalem.

Solomon's Temple was destroyed in 586 BC. The Second Temple, initially completed in 516 BC and totally refurnished and enlarged by King Herod beginning in 18 BC, was destroyed as well, in AD 70. Yet Jesus mentioned the existence of "the holy place" in a future Temple when He told His

19

disciples about the events of the last days and the Great Tribulation. He warned that "when ye therefore shall see the abomination of desolation, spoken of by Daniel the prophet, stand in the holy place, (whoso readeth, let him understand:) then let them which be in Judaea flee into the mountains" (Matthew 24:15–16). Jesus' prophecy echoed that of the prophet Daniel, who indicated that the "abomination that maketh desolate" would stand in the Temple of God in Jerusalem (see Daniel 11:31; 12:11). Both prophecies suggest that the Third Temple will be built before the Antichrist comes to power and takes control of Europe and the surrounding Mediterranean nations.

Satan will spiritually defile the Holy Place of the rebuilt Temple by directing his Antichrist to violate the Holy of Holies at the beginning of the last three and a half years of the Tribulation. The False Prophet, the Antichrist's partner, will then demand that the Antichrist be worshiped as "god" in the rebuilt Temple.

Controversy over Rebuilding the Temple

Among the ongoing tragedies of the Middle East is that both Arabs and Jews claim the right of possession of the Holy Land, the city of Jerusalem, and the Temple Mount. In just about any current news report involving the conflict between Israel and its Arab enemies, the ancient, walled Old City of Jerusalem plays a prominent role. God told His prophets thousands of years ago that the final battle for the soul and destiny of mankind will be decided in Jerusalem, whose name literally means "city of peace," the city where the coming Messiah will establish His eternal throne.

The Third Temple will be built on what is the most passionately contested piece of real estate on earth. Not only is this rebuilding prophesied in Scripture, but today rabbis, researchers, archaeologists, and other interested parties are drawing up detailed architectural plans, re-creating precious vessels to be used in Temple worship, and searching for the lost treasures of the ancient Temple. Incredible progress has been made recently in locating, gathering, and in some cases re-creating the necessary vessels, utensils, and other sacred objects that will be necessary to reinstate sacred worship and animal sacrifice.

Key figures of the Orthodox Jewish leadership in Israel have finally thrown their support behind the many efforts currently under way to prepare for building the Third

Temple. The progress, extent, and timing of these preparations will be examined in later chapters of this book.

Control of the Temple Mount

After Israel's stunning victory over the Arab armies during the Six-Day War in June 1967, Israeli defense minister General Moshe Dayan went to the Al-Aqsa Mosque to meet with the five leaders of the Supreme Muslim Religious Council. The council had exercised control over the Temple Mount during nearly twenty years of Jordanian military control of the eastern portion of Jerusalem, from Israel's 1948 War of Independence until the Six-Day War. The meeting between Dayan and the Muslim leaders established Israel's religious and political policy concerning the Temple Mount, a policy that remains unchanged today. Dayan, a nonreligious Jew, did not appreciate the profound historical and spiritual significance of the Temple Mount and thus relinquished administrative control to the Arabs. He hoped the generosity of this gesture would be appreciated. Unfortunately, they interpreted it as an indication of the weakness of Israel's resolve to possess and hold their holiest place of worship, the Temple Mount.

Dayan ordered the Israeli flag that Jewish soldiers had affixed to the golden dome removed from the Dome of the Rock. His further concessions surrendered administrative control of the Temple Mount to the Supreme Muslim Religious Council, a Jordanian-controlled Muslim trust known as the Waqf. Though Jews would be permitted limited access to the Temple Mount area, all prayer or reading of Scripture by Jews and Christians was prohibited.

The Temple Mount remains at the center of Israeli-Arab tensions, with Arab authorities continuing to exercise administrative control over Israel's most sacred site. However, God has called on His people to rebuild the Temple. Not only is this critical development commanded by God, but the Scriptures reveal that the Temple will be rebuilt before the Messiah returns to earth.

In the chapters that follow, we will look not only at the advancing plans and preparations to rebuild the Temple, but also at a number of closely related developments, such as the training of Levite priests, the recovery of long-lost Temple treasures, developments in locating the ark of the covenant and returning it to Jerusalem, and the discovery of ancient vessels and artifacts that are required for Temple sacrifice and worship. With a new Sanhedrin Court now in place, with some five hundred Levites being trained in the requirements of Temple animal sacrifice, and with critical lost treasures from the Second Temple being located and returned to Jerusalem, it is no longer just a dream that the Temple of God will once again stand on the Temple Mount.

After nineteen centuries of praying and waiting, the Jews have finally been given the historic task of making their ancient dreams come true. The building of the Third Temple will commence much sooner than most people expect. The generation alive today will see the Temple of God once again standing in Jerusalem, and the King of Israel — the returning Messiah — ruling from the throne of David!

■ ■ ■ ■

ONE:
PREPARING THE WAY
FOR THE THIRD
TEMPLE

RECENT DISCOVERIES HAVE REMOVED
SEVERAL MAJOR OBSTACLES
TO REBUILDING

■ ■ ■ ■

My tabernacle also shall be with them:
yea, I will be their God,
and they shall be my people.

Ezekiel 37:27

The great rabbi Moses Maimonides (AD 1200), affectionately called Rambam, taught that the study of the Temple has eternal significance because it reveals the nature of God and His relationship to Israel. Maimonides noted that the 613 *mitzvot,* or commandments, of the Torah include God's direct command to build the Temple: "And let them make me a sanctuary; that I may dwell among them. According to all that I shew thee, after the pattern of the tabernacle, and the pattern of all the instruments thereof, even so shall ye make it" (Exodus 25:8–9).

God gave Moses His blueprints, a pattern for the Tabernacle that would ensure the earthly sanctuary would duplicate as far as humanly possible the heavenly sanctuary. Both the Tabernacle created in the wilderness after the Exodus and the magnificent Temple built by King Solomon were patterned after God's eternal sanctuary in the heavens — even to the details of the worship instruments and sacred vessels.

Maimonides, in his influential study *Hilchos Bais HaBechirah* (The Laws of God's Chosen House), pointed out that the Temple had two distinct purposes. First, it revealed to mankind the Divine Presence. (The Shekinah Glory of God dwelt above the mercy seat of the ark of the covenant.) The second purpose of the Temple was to serve as God's chosen place for offering divine sacrifices, as outlined in the book of Exodus. The Lord commanded Moses to "speak unto the children of Israel, that they bring me an offering: of every man that giveth it willingly with his heart ye shall take my offering" (Exodus 25:2).

Ever since 586 BC, when the Babylonian army destroyed Solomon's Temple, the Jews have read the book of Lamentations on the anniversary of the Temple's destruction. They read Jeremiah's words of lament and recall the tragic destruction of the magnificent golden and marble Temple. After the Roman army burned the Second Temple in AD 70 — on the ninth day of Av, *the very same day of the year* that Solomon's Temple was destroyed — it was thought that the Temple had been lost forever. With no

Temple standing in Jerusalem, the Jewish religious leadership was left with only the synagogue, the Torah, and rabbinical commentary writings in the Talmud to express their love for God's holy name. However, the Lord prophesied that in the last days the exiles would return to the Promised Land to rebuild Jerusalem and the Temple. "But in the last days it shall come to pass, that the mountain of the house of the LORD shall be established in the top of the mountains, and it shall be exalted above the hills; and people shall flow unto it" (Micah 4:1). The "mountain of the house of the LORD" is a widely understood reference to the sacred Temple.

After nineteen centuries of exile, the Jewish people returned to Israel to possess the Holy Land and Jerusalem, the Holy City. But since both the Jews and the Arabs claim the right to control the city of Jerusalem, any talk of rebuilding the Temple is cause for profound concern throughout the Middle East.

SETTING THE STAGE FOR END-TIMES EVENTS

Researchers for the Temple Institute and the religious leadership in Israel have made astounding progress in their preparations to rebuild the Temple. With plans moving forward to resume the sacred worship rituals in a rebuilt Temple, a major prophetic signpost is in place pointing to the fact that the Messiah's return is at hand. This is consistent with numerous prophecies that indicate the Third Temple will be built before Satan's coming dictator, the Antichrist, appears and takes political control of the ten nations of the revived Roman Empire and then the nations of the world.

Daniel foresaw in his vision of the seventy weeks that this coming world dictator would make a "covenant" (or peace treaty) with Israel (the "many") for seven years (see Daniel 9:24–27). The ancient Jews used *heptads,* or "weeks" of years, to indicate a period of seven years' duration, just as we use *decade* to refer to a period of ten years' duration. Three and a half years after the initial covenant signing, the dictator would break the treaty and enter the Temple to defile it. The prophet states: "He shall cause the sacrifice and the oblation to cease" (Daniel 9:27). Animal sacrifices have not occurred in Jerusalem since the summer of AD 70, when Titus's legions burned the Second Temple to the ground. Obviously, the Antichrist cannot stop the daily sacrifice unless, prior to this time, the Levitical

animal sacrificial system has been reinstated. Therefore, at some point in the
future, the Jews will renew the sacrificial
system on the Temple Mount.

In prophesying about the Great Tribulation, Jesus referred to the future Third
Temple and the wicked acts of the Antichrist
(see Matthew 24:15). The abomination of
desolation, referred to by both the prophet
Daniel and Jesus, is the ultimate spiritual
defiling of the Holy Place of the Temple.
Satan will demand that the Antichrist must
be worshiped as "god" in the Temple. For
this prophecy to be fulfilled, of course, the
Third Temple must have been built (see
photograph).

In his second letter to the church at Thes-
salonica, Paul advised that the Lord would
not return until "that man of sin," the
Antichrist, is finally revealed — "the son of
perdition; who opposeth and exalteth himself above all that is called God, or that is
worshipped; so that he as God sitteth in the
temple of God, shewing himself that he is
God" (2 Thessalonians 2:3–4). Paul is not
the only early Christian writer who referred
to a future Temple. Lactantius wrote about
a rebuilt Temple that would stand in the
last days prior to Christ's return. In his
book *The Divine Institutes,* he described the

seven-year Tribulation period and the persecution that will be brought about by the Antichrist: "Then he will attempt to destroy the temple of God and persecute the righteous people; and there will be distress and tribulation, such as there never has been from the beginning of the world."[1]

Another early church theologian, Victorinus, also wrote about the Third Temple. His *Commentary on the Apocalypse* explored the prophecies found in the book of Revelation. Victorinus wrote about the False Prophet, the partner of the coming Antichrist, saying the False Prophet will place an image, or statue, of the Antichrist in the rebuilt Temple. Victorinus quoted Revelation 13:13, stating, "And he shall make fire come down from heaven in the sight of men." Then Victorinus added regarding the False Prophet: "He shall cause also that a golden image of Antichrist shall be placed in the Temple at Jerusalem. . . . 'And he shall place,' says he, 'his temple within Samaria [an ancient name for Israel], upon the illustrious and holy mountain that is at Jerusalem.' "[2]

Some Christian commentators have suggested that the Antichrist will lead the project to rebuild the Temple. However, the evidence from Scripture causes me to take

This closeup view of a model of the Second Temple reflects what the Third Temple will look like when plans for rebuilding move forward.

quite a different view. While numerous prophecies describe the Antichrist defiling the Temple, John refers to the sanctuary as the Temple of God. "And there was given me a reed like unto a rod: and the angel stood, saying, Rise, and measure the temple of God, and the altar, and them that worship therein" (Revelation 11:1). In addition, when the apostle Paul wrote about the Antichrist being revealed, he referred to evil acts that would be carried out in "the temple of God" (see 2 Thessalonians 2:4). These passages strongly suggest that the Jews in genuine worship of God will build the Third Temple and that the Antichrist

33

will later defile it during the Tribulation. Fortunately, the Word of God reveals that when the Messiah comes, "then shall the sanctuary be cleansed" (Daniel 8:14).

One of the greatest of the early church writers, Irenaeus, taught that the new Temple would be a genuine Temple built by the religious Jews. Citing 2 Thessalonians 2:4, he stated that "the Apostle himself, speaking in his own person, distinctly called it the temple of God."[3]

Further, in his book *Against Heresies,* Irenaeus affirmed his understanding of the Scriptures' prophecies about animal sacrifice being reinstated in a future Temple. He cited Daniel's words in Daniel 9:27, stating, "the sacrifice and the libation shall be taken away, and the abomination of desolation [shall] be brought into the Temple: even unto the consummation of the time shall the desolation be complete."[4] Again, for these prophetic events to occur, the Third Temple must be rebuilt by the Jews as a legitimate Temple of God.

DEBATE SURROUNDING THE TEMPLE'S LOCATION

One of the most problematic obstacles to the rebuilding of the Temple is the location of the famous Muslim shrine known as the

Dome of the Rock. This beautiful structure was erected by Caliph Abdal-Malik in AD 691. For almost thirteen centuries people have believed that this shrine was built directly over the site of the original Temple of Solomon. If that were the case, the Dome of the Rock would need to be removed before the Third Temple could be built. Some students of prophecy suggest that a disaster such as an earthquake or a missile strike would be necessary to remove the Muslim shrine to allow the Temple to be built.

But what if this assumption is in error? What if the Dome of the Rock does *not* occupy the location of Solomon's Temple? If that were the case, then the Third Temple could be built at the correct location without disturbing the Muslim shrine. And that is exactly what I believe prophecy tells us.

In a vision of the second half of the seven-year Tribulation, the apostle John was told by the angel to measure the Temple of God and the altar (Revelation 11:1). But in a significant statement, the angel tells him not to measure the Court of the Gentiles: "But the court which is without the temple leave out, and measure it not; for it is given unto the Gentiles: and the holy city shall they tread under foot forty and two months"

(Revelation 11:2). John saw in his vision that there would be a period after the rebuilding of the Temple in which a part of the Temple Mount known as the Court of the Gentiles would still be given over to the Gentiles (the Arab Muslims) for forty-two months until Christ returns to set up His eternal kingdom.

Under Israeli law, the legal principle of status quo demands that any significant religious site in Israel (Jewish, Christian, or Muslim) cannot be altered in a major way, regardless of events. This principle was enacted into law by the Islamic Turkish authorities during their governorship, reinforced by the British Mandate (1921–48), and confirmed in Israel's basic laws since 1948. Thus, if the Dome of the Rock were ever damaged, Israeli law would demand that it be rebuilt as it was originally constructed. No one is suggesting that Israel would demolish the Dome of the Rock to clear the location needed for rebuilding the Temple. And in light of John's prophecy, we see that the Dome of the Rock will remain where it is, at least during the Tribulation.

Archaeological research has enabled Jewish authorities to determine that the original site of Solomon's Temple, and hence the location where the Third Temple will be built, is in a wide-open area directly north of the Dome of the Rock. In the months following the recapture of the Temple Mount in June 1967, Israeli archaeologists began digging a nine-hundred-yard-long tunnel in a northerly direction along the Western Wall from the area known as Wilson's Arch toward the northwest corner of the Temple Mount. This tunnel is almost sixty-five feet below the level of the present-day streets of Jerusalem. It has become known as the Rabbi's Tunnel because, after 1967, Orthodox rabbis who desired to someday rebuild the Temple used the tunnel to approach the entrance to the ancient site of the Holy of Holies for prayer.

Over the last two decades I have visited numerous hidden areas beneath the Temple Mount and have seen where Jewish archaeologists have exposed the original Herodian foundation stones far beneath the level that one stands upon when visiting the Western Wall plaza. Some of these gigantic blocks of limestone measure forty-six feet by twenty feet by ten feet. Each one can weigh up to one thousand tons, and the foundation stones are fitted so perfectly together that it is impossible to place even a razor blade between them.

Some scholars believe these are the foundation stones that were placed at the deepest level in the Western Wall under the direction of King Solomon almost three thousand years ago. If this is correct, King Herod used the deepest surviving layer of foundation stones. He ordered his craftsmen to frame these stones with a quarter-inch indentation around the edge to match his stones (ashlars). They built up the foundation until it reached the surface and higher, reaching a level near the present Old City wall (rebuilt by Suleiman the Magnificent in AD 1542). It is fascinating to note that modern machinery, including cranes and helicopters, would be unable to transport these one-thousand-ton stones the one-mile distance from the quarry where they were excavated to their ultimate location, sixty-five feet beneath the current surface of the Temple Mount.

Further evidence of the site of Solomon's Temple was unearthed in the early 1980s with the discovery of a previously unknown gate beneath the Temple Mount. Several hundred feet north of Wilson's Arch, as archaeologists extended the Western Wall tunnel northward, they uncovered an ancient gate that led eastward into passages beneath the Temple Mount that had been built by King Herod in the time of the

Second Temple. Of particular interest is a passage that leads directly toward the location of the Beautiful Gate and the sealed Eastern Gate of the Temple Mount. This strongly suggests that the location of the First and Second Temples lies north of the Dome of the Rock. An interesting photo I took from the Garden of Gethsemane, directly opposite the closed Eastern Gate (also called the Golden Gate), shows that the Dome of the Rock was built on a site more than one hundred fifty feet to the south of the original Temple site, which is directly west of the Eastern Gate (see photograph).

Explorations Underneath the Temple Mount

The underground Western Gate was filled with rocks and debris from the destruction of the Second Temple. As the debris was cleared away, the Israeli team saw that this ancient gate led into a complex network of tunnels, some of which led directly eastward under the site of the Second Temple. This confirmed Jewish legends and ancient writings that the area underneath the Temple Mount was honeycombed with secret passages and thirty-nine cisterns — some as large as a cathedral — as reported by the

This photograph, taken from a location east of the Temple Mount, shows the closed Eastern Gate (center). The Dome of the Rock is located beyond the Eastern Gate and to the south of the site of the First and Second Temples.

Jewish historian Flavius Josephus.

When the Western Gate was discovered, Muslim authorities demanded that it be permanently sealed with concrete. In response, the Israeli government agreed to temporarily limit archaeological exploration of the religiously sensitive area. Several of the individuals who entered this tunnel, including Rabbi Yehuda Getz, the chief rabbi of the Western Wall, later described what they had seen from a distance of fifty yards. These men believed they had identified some of the golden worship vessels used

40

in the Second Temple. However, they were not able to examine these objects due to Islamic opposition to their continued access to the tunnel and, more important, due to their fear of inadvertently defiling the Holy of Holies of the ancient Temple.

Further evidence confirming the original location of the ancient Temple is the discovery of the layout of a series of underground cisterns, treasure rooms, and guardrooms that lie beneath the Temple Mount. I have seen several of these huge cisterns, which can each hold hundreds of thousands of gallons of water. Together, the thirty-nine cisterns, cut out of the natural limestone that lies beneath the Temple Mount, can hold more than twelve million gallons of water. Water storage was essential because water was used in cleansing the Temple sanctuary, and vast stores of water were needed in the event of a prolonged attack. Additional storage structures held enormous supplies of grain, enough to feed the people for a siege lasting a dozen years or more. No other city in the ancient world was as well prepared to withstand a siege.

The Location of the Holy of Holies
Yet another confirmation of the true site of the ancient Temple is the above-ground

location of a small Arabic cupola known as Qubbat al-Arwah, or the Dome of the Spirits. This structure is located more than one hundred fifty feet to the north of the Dome of the Rock and sits precisely on an imaginary line drawn in a westerly direction from the sealed Eastern Gate toward the opposite Western Wall of the Temple Mount. It is an open structure with columns and a small dome built on a foundation stone composed of the bedrock of Mount Moriah.

The Dome of the Spirits (also known as the Dome of the Tablets) stands isolated on

This Muslim shrine, known as the Dome of the Spirits, is thought to incorporate the foundation stone that supported the ark of the covenant in the ancient Holy of Holies.

the site surrounding the flat foundation stone. The structure's two names may well reveal ancient knowledge that this stone is, in fact, the foundation stone that supported the ark of the covenant. The ark contained the tablets of the Law and was kept in the Holy of Holies in Solomon's Temple. The *Mishneh Torah* (Moses Maimonides' authoritative commentary on the Temple) records that there was a foundation stone in Solomon's Temple known as *even ha-shetiyah* and that the ark of the covenant rested on that stone. But in the Second Temple, the foundation stone stood unadorned in the Holy of Holies because the ark of the covenant had already been removed from Jerusalem (see photograph).[5]

In 1896, only a short distance southeast of the Dome of the Spirits, British archaeologists located a cistern that in ancient times was positioned between the Temple porch and the altar of sacrifice. This pit was apparently designed to contain the liquid libation offerings connected with the Temple services. The discovery of this cistern helps identify the location of the Holy of Holies in relation to the altar of sacrifice and further confirms the location of the Holy of Holies as being north of the Dome of the Rock. The Third Temple can be built on the exact location of Solomon's Temple, with the Holy of Holies occupying its original location surrounding the ancient foundation stone that held the ark of the covenant.

In view of this research, it becomes clear that Israel could rebuild the Temple without disturbing the Dome of the Rock. In addition, a scale model of the Second Temple — including the Court of the Gentiles — shows that building the Third Temple without this court, based on the prophecy of Revelation 11:1–2, would leave both the Dome of the Rock and the Al-Aqsa Mosque undisturbed. Both structures sit in the area that previously was occupied by the Court of the Gentiles. The Third Temple would lie more than one hundred fifty feet to the north of the Muslim shrines.

PREPARATIONS TO REBUILD THE TEMPLE

Since the modern State of Israel was founded in 1948, a number of Israeli groups have been putting in place the plans and practical steps necessary to rebuild a Temple on the Temple Mount. The television program *60 Minutes* reported in 1985 that rabbinical students in Jerusalem were studying the reintroduction of the ancient Jewish rites of sacrifice on the Temple Mount.[6]

I have seen and photographed the yeshiva

(Jewish theological college) where these students were studying. The school, led by the late Rabbi Shlomo Goren, stands within five hundred yards of the Western Wall of the ancient Temple. In 1967, Goren was the chief rabbi of the Israel Defense Forces. He blew the shofar, the ram's horn, immediately after Israel recaptured the Western Wall in the Six-Day War. This conquest returned the Temple Mount to Jewish control for the first time in almost two thousand years.

Plans and preparations are under way on other fronts. An Orthodox Jewish group calling itself Netemanei Har Habayit, the "Faithful of the Temple Mount," has built a detailed model of the Temple. A fund has been established to collect donations for the rebuilding project. And reliable sources in Israel have told me that over the last century, millions of dollars have been set aside in wills and trusts by Jews who want to help finance the Temple reconstruction.

On February 11, 1996, the Temple Mount and Land of Israel Faithful Movement, an Orthodox Jewish group that wants to rebuild the Temple, hired the Gallup Organization to survey Israeli attitudes regarding the rebuilding of the Temple in our generation. The survey found that 58 percent of those polled agreed that Israel should proceed with plans to rebuild the Temple. It is interesting that the highest level of support was found among younger Israelis.[7]

The Temple Mount is in Israeli hands, and the exact site for rebuilding has been identified. The area where the Third Temple will be built is unoccupied. A fund has been created, and a priesthood made up of Jews from the tribe of Levi is in training as authorized by the newly reconstituted Sanhedrin Court, the highest court of Jewish law in Israel. The path has largely been cleared for the momentous events to take place just as they were described by the prophets. The approaching footsteps of the Messiah can be heard in these exciting events.

■ ■ ■ ■

Two:
The Glory of
Jerusalem's Temple

RE-CREATING THE SANCTUARY OF
GOD ON EARTH

■ ■ ■ ■

Then Solomon began to build the house
   of the LORD
at Jerusalem in mount Moriah,
where the LORD appeared unto David his
   father.

2 Chronicles 3:1

Not in the influential city of Antioch, not in the fabled city of Alexandria, and not even in the magnificence of imperial Rome would a person living in the days of Jesus encounter a structure that would take his breath away as much as the golden Temple in Jerusalem. The dazzling beauty of the sanctuary, ornamented in marble and gold, far exceeded any other religious building or government structure anywhere in the world. From the time of King Solomon, three thousand years ago, until the present day, there has never existed an edifice to match the wonders of Solomon's Temple or its successor, the Second Temple, built by King Herod.

In response to God's command to Israel to build a sanctuary, King David wanted to honor the Lord by building a permanent Temple to take the place of the movable Tabernacle. As a result of his many victories

49

in battle, David was in possession of a vast number of slaves as well as an enormous amount of captured gold and silver. He intended to build the greatest Temple the world had ever seen. However, God declared that David would not be allowed to build the sacred sanctuary because he had spent his life in violence.[1] Because of David's career as "a man of blood" (both in war and in plotting the death of Uriah, Bathsheba's husband), the privilege of building the Temple would pass to his son King Solomon (see 1 Chronicles 17:11–12; 28:3).

As a result of God's prohibition, David accumulated the materials required to build a magnificent Temple. His son Solomon used the materials, precious metals, and vast wealth to complete the massive construction project. It was the crowning achievement of Solomon's reign.

SOLOMON'S UNEQUALED BUILDING PROJECT

Even though God prevented David from building the Temple, the Lord gave him precise blueprints for the structure, including its vast subterranean cisterns, treasuries, and tunnels. Perhaps to avoid any confusion or misunderstanding, God supplied the plans in writing: "All this, said David, the LORD made me understand in writing by his hand upon me, even all the works of this pattern" (1 Chronicles 28:19). The Scriptures are silent about the details of these written plans; therefore, we should not speculate beyond what is written in the Word of God. The New Testament tells us that the priests and the Temple "serve unto the example and shadow of heavenly things, as Moses was admonished of God when he was about to make the tabernacle: for, See, saith he, that thou make all things according to the pattern shewed to thee in the mount" (Hebrews 8:5).

At the appropriate time, David presented Solomon the plans for building the Temple: "Then David gave to Solomon his son the pattern of the porch, and of the houses thereof, and of the treasuries thereof, and of the upper chambers thereof, and of the inner parlours thereof, and of the place of the mercy seat, and the pattern of all that he had by the spirit, of the courts of the house of the LORD" (1 Chronicles 28:11–12). The plans of both the Tabernacle (used for five centuries beginning with the Exodus) and the Temple itself were patterned after the eternal sanctuary of God in heaven. It's interesting to note that the dimensions of Solomon's Temple were precisely double the dimensions of the

Tabernacle used in the wilderness.

In building the Temple, Solomon followed God's instructions pertaining to the unique method of construction. God prohibited the use of any iron tools in the assembly of the materials on the Temple Mount: "There was neither hammer nor axe nor any tool of iron heard in the house, while it was in building" (1 Kings 6:7). Some rabbis have interpreted this reference to mean that no iron was to be used at all during the preparation of the stones, while many believe the injunction applied only to the final assembly of the quarried stones. Either way, it's clear that the Lord established the sanctity of the Holy Mount from the first day of the Temple's construction.

The stones were quarried from three locations: the Royal Caverns beneath the present-day Muslim Quarter in the northern portion of the Old City; the quarries located near the present-day Knesset (Israel's parliament buildings); and a quarry in Lebanon, from which the stones were transported on rafts to Joppa. The stones from Lebanon were a contribution from King Hiram. The historian Flavius Josephus noted: "Now, therefore, the king laid the foundations of the temple very deep in the ground, and the materials were strong stones, and such as would resist the force of time; these were to unite themselves with the earth, and become a basis and a sure foundation for that superstructure."[2]

The Jewish sages documented a curious tradition that many miracles occurred during the building of the First Temple. One of the most intriguing is the claim that none of the many thousands of skilled workers died during the seven-year construction project. The tradition stated that after the dedication of the sanctuary, God caused all the workers to die and immediately enter paradise as their reward for participating in the sacred project. This curious tradition claims that the death of the workers also prevented any profane king from employing the highly skilled craftsman to build a palace or temple that would glorify any king or false god.[3]

BUILDING MATERIALS FOR THE TEMPLE

Though King David could not personally build the Temple, he did gather the enormous amounts of material and gold required for such a mammoth project. The Scriptures record the staggering amount of the treasure of gold and silver that was expended on the Temple's construction.

Now, behold, in my trouble I have prepared

for the house of the LORD an hundred thousand talents of gold, and a thousand thousand talents of silver; and of brass and iron without weight; for it is in abundance: timber also and stone have I prepared; and thou mayest add thereto. Moreover there are workmen with thee in abundance, hewers and workers of stone and timber, and all manner of cunning men for every manner of work. (1 Chronicles 22:14–15)

After years of conquest of surrounding kingdoms and the annual collection of tribute, David's accumulated treasury included one hundred thousand talents of gold (three thousand tons, an amount that exceeds the worldwide production of gold in 2006). Calculating the value based on the price of gold as of this writing ($670 per ounce), the gold used in constructing the Temple equaled an astonishing $64 billion. In addition, David gave Solomon one million talents of silver (equal to thirty thousand tons and with a current value of nearly $13 billion). This is equal to one and a half times the current annual production of silver throughout the world.[4]

Josephus records that the Temple's walls and floors were covered in gold. "He also laid the floor of the temple with plates of gold; and he added doors to the gate of the temple, agreeable to the measure of the height of the wall, but in breadth twenty cubits, and on them he glued gold plates. And, to say all in one word, he left no part of the temple, neither internal nor external, but what was covered with gold."[5]

The Bible and ancient Jewish commentaries paint a picture of the glorious beauty of Solomon's Temple. The interior ceiling was 180 feet long and 90 feet wide and rose to a height of 50 feet. The highest point on the Temple's exterior structure was 207 feet. According to the Jewish commentary known as the *Tanach,* the length of the Temple was 180 feet (60 cubits), and the breadth was 60 feet (20 cubits, see *Tanach* 3:3). The Temple was wider at the entrance porch (90 feet), but the rear section measured 60 feet wide. This is using a cubit measurement of 36 inches. (There were several different lengths of the ancient cubit.)

Solomon requested that King Hiram of Tyre deliver vast quantities of costly cedar from Lebanon. To pay for building materials from the north, Solomon transferred twenty small towns in northern Galilee to King Hiram in compensation for enormous shipments of cedar and quarried stone, plus the use of skilled craftsmen (see 1 Kings 9:11). Solomon made special use of the skills of one of Hiram's craftsmen who was a gifted sculptor (see 2 Chronicles 2:13–14). The man was a brilliant artist and builder and was responsible for a great deal of the final craftsmanship that was revealed in the Temple's gold and brass ornamentation. Intriguingly, this sculptor was descended from the tribe of Dan. He shared the ancestry of the amazingly talented craftsman Aholiab, the artist who had constructed the worship vessels for Moses in the wilderness five centuries earlier.

To accomplish the massive construction project, Solomon imposed forced labor on tens of thousands of slaves as well as citizens of Israel. He drafted Israelites to serve the nation for work periods up to one month. Every month Solomon appointed some thirty-three hundred new overseers to supervise the construction (see *Tanach* 5:27–30).

THE COURTS OF THE TEMPLE

The major entrance to the Temple was through the Royal Porch, which featured a set of 162 marble pillars arranged in a west-east line across the southern portion of the Temple Mount. Each of the four rows of pillars (including one row of columns built into the southern wall) consisted of forty massive columns, with an additional two at the entrance to the Royal Porch. Each Corinthian marble pillar was a monolith quarried from a single block of stone 37.5 feet in height. Gigantic columns in the central nave (each one 45 feet wide) reached 100 feet in the air.[6]

The Royal Porch actually contained a number of porches, or cloisters, that encompassed the huge expanse of the Court of the Temple, commonly known as the Court of the Gentiles. We read in the New Testament of Jesus dialoguing with the rabbis at age twelve and later of Christ and His apostles teaching in the Temple, and those events undoubtedly occurred among these cloisters of the Temple.

When a Jewish worshiper entered the Temple complex, he would enter on the right and exit on the left. The Court of the Gentiles (called by the Jews the "mountain of the house") was a square courtyard measuring seven hundred fifty feet on each side.[7] This area was paved with costly and beautiful variegated marble. All the Temple courts contained benches for worshipers to use. That was an important provision, considering the Temple Mount could accommodate as many as 250,000 worshipers at one time. In our generation up to 250,000 Muslim worshipers have gathered on the Noble Sanctuary (the Temple Mount) for major Islamic festivals.

The Temple walls were high, and the drop in elevation on the east side from the Temple Mount to the floor of the Kidron Valley equaled a depth of 450 feet, measured from the pinnacle of the Temple. This apparently was the spot described in Luke's gospel where Jesus rejected Satan's temptation to drop Himself off the Temple pin-

The Second Temple

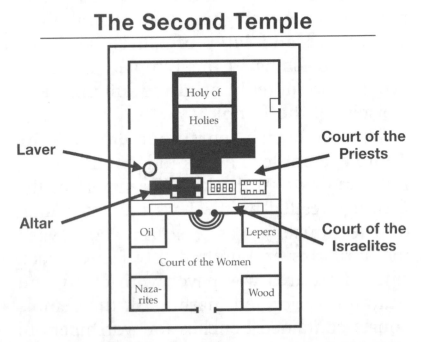

This diagram shows the layout of the interior of the Second Temple.

nacle to the valley below (see Luke 4:9–12).

Beyond the Court of the Gentiles, the more sacred courts of the Temple were constructed on higher and higher levels (see diagram). In the mid-1800s Turkish authorities found an ancient engraved inscription near the Temple Mount that warned Gentiles not to proceed beyond the Court of the Gentiles on pain of death. This inscription confirms the account in the book of Acts (21:28–30) about the crowd attacking the apostle Paul when they erroneously thought he had violated the Temple regulations that prohibited Gentiles from entering the sanctuary. From the Court of the Gentiles, fourteen steps (each nine inches in height) led a worshiper up to the chel, a fifteen-foot wide terrace that encircled the inside wall of the Temple structure.

The Temple sanctuary itself was composed of three individual courts: the Court of the Women, the Court of the Israelites, and the Court of the Priests (open only to priests and those offering sacrifices). This design was constructed upon a platform, with each court rising higher as a person approached the area of the Holy of Holies. This was intended to reinforce in the worshiper the truth that each step forward and upward led one closer to the Shekinah Glory of

God, which was present in the Holy of Holies. We need to remember, however, that after the destruction of Solomon's Temple in 586 BC, the ark of the covenant was no longer in the Holy of Holies. (We will discuss this in detail in chapter 8.)

From the terrace (the chel), nine gates led into the Temple. The most magnificent was the eastern-facing gate, called the Beautiful Gate, which was the principal entrance to the Temple structure. A worshiper would ascend twelve steps from the chel and then enter through the Beautiful Gate, which was constructed of brass from Corinth. Jewish tradition claims that the massive brass double doors were so heavy that twenty strong Levite priests were required to open and close them.

On the north side of the central Temple structure was a chamber known as the Hall of Hewn Stones. This was the chamber where the Sanhedrin, the highest court of Jewish law, met. The Sanhedrin deliberated on significant cases that related to sacred law. A familiar example from the New Testament is the trial of Jesus, when the Sanhedrin convened to consider His unusual claims that He was God's anointed One, the promised Messiah.

THE MEANING AND USE OF
THE TEMPLE COURTS

As a worshiper entered the Temple super-structure, he or she would ascend using a series of magnificent marble staircases. Having entered through the Court of the Gentiles, the worshiper would take a staircase directly to the front of the Temple itself, leading to the Court of the Women, then higher yet to the Court of the Israelites, and finally into the more sacred Court of the Priests. In this highest structure, the priests performed their worship duties.

The Court of the Women included four chambers. Any Jews (men or women) were permitted to enter this court. The entrance from the Court of the Women into the Court of the Israelites was the massive Gate of Nicanor. According to Jewish tradition, the gate was named for the wealthy man who donated the costly brass gate. Fifteen steps upward led through the gate, and on the Feast of Tabernacles, Levite priests would stand on these steps and sing the fifteen "Psalms of Degrees" (Psalms 120–34).

The Court of the Israelites was restricted to Jewish males. A low marble structure eighteen inches high separated it from the Court of the Priests, an area restricted to priests and Jewish worshipers of both genders who were there to offer sacrifices.[8] The Court of the Priests was quite large, measuring approximately two hundred sixty-five feet long by two hundred two feet wide. Animal sacrifices were carried out daily in the Court of the Priests.

THE ALTAR

The altar stood in the Court of the Priests just before the steps leading into the Holy Place. The altar was constructed of unhewn stones that were whitewashed every six months to eliminate the inevitable discoloration caused by the blood of animal sacrifices. The altar formed a square measuring approximately forty-eight feet on each side and stood almost fifteen feet high. Four hollow "horns" rose approximately eighteen inches higher than the top surface of the altar at each corner. The horns were used to receive the drink offerings, including the special offering of water from the Pool of Siloam that was poured into the horns during the Feast of Tabernacles.

The vast number of animals sacrificed during the major days of liturgical sacrifice (Passover, Pentecost, and Tabernacles) produced an enormous amount of blood and waste, which had to be removed from the altar area. A complex system of tunnels and aqueducts brought a massive amount of water to the Temple from huge reservoirs surrounding Jerusalem. The aqueduct was designed using sophisticated engineering that staggers the imagination; the tunnel system transported water over a forty-mile course, and it was constructed almost three thousand years ago! The tunnels were drilled through mountains. Aqueducts were built around mountains, and segments of the watercourse had a drop in elevation of only a few inches per mile. However, the system succeeded in carrying water dozens of miles from near Bethlehem, Etham, and Hebron to the Temple Mount in Jerusalem.

It has been calculated that more than ten million gallons of water were stored in the system of thirty-nine cisterns located in subterranean chambers deep beneath the Temple Mount. The greatest of these cisterns, known as the Great Sea, alone held more than two million gallons of water.

The water was used to flush the blood and other animal waste materials through an elaborate system of drainage tunnels that lay beneath the surface flagstones of the Temple. Animal waste products were flushed eastward to outlets deep in the Kidron Valley. Years of accumulated waste material produced an incredibly rich compost that was treasured by the gardeners of ancient Jerusalem, according to Jewish tradition.

CONSECRATION OF THE FIRST TEMPLE

When Solomon completed construction of the First Temple, he prayed that "all the people of the earth may know thy name, to fear thee, as do thy people Israel; and that they may know that this house, which I have builded, is called by thy name" (1 Kings 8:43). He consecrated the Temple during an elaborate service when the Levite priests brought the ark of the covenant into the Holy of Holies. Fire descended from heaven to light the altar to demonstrate that God had chosen this sanctuary to be His house of worship on earth (see 2 Chronicles 7:1–2).

The Scriptures record that the priests sacrificed 22,000 oxen and 120,000 sheep during the festival of dedication. The meat from the animals would have been distributed to the priests, Levites, and the people who came to the festival. Nothing was wasted. If the recorded number of sacrificed animals seems impossibly high, remember that the Muslim leader Khalif Moktader is reliably reported by the explorer Sir Richard Burton, who secretly visited Mecca in disguise, to have sacrificed 40,000 camels and 50,000 sheep during a major Islamic festival in the 1870s.[9]

KING HEROD REBUILDS THE TEMPLE

When the Jewish exiles returned from Babylon in 536 BC under the decree of the Persian king Cyrus, they found Jerusalem and the Temple Mount in ruins. After they had been in Jerusalem for two decades, the exiles finished rebuilding Solomon's Temple. But due to the limitations imposed by their foreign rulers, the Persian kings Cyrus and Darius, the rebuilt Temple was only a dim shadow of the former one and its glory.

However, the Temple would once again regain its magnificence. Around 18 BC. King Herod began an immense building project to reconstruct and enlarge the Second Temple to rival the glory of Solomon's Temple. The work was so extensive that the Second Temple was still being built during the ministry of Jesus forty-six years after construction began. Herod, known as the Great Builder, constructed a number of excellent buildings, including those in Caesarea, Hebron, Masada, Jericho, and most of all in the capital city, Jerusalem. However, his greatest architectural contribution was the construction of the Second Temple. Herod's enlarged Temple Mount was one hundred yards longer north to south than Solomon's Temple.[10]

This is how the historian Flavius Josephus described Herod's building project: "Accordingly in the fifteenth year of his reign, he [King Herod] restored the existing sanctuary and round it enclosed an area double the former size, keeping no account of its costs and achieving magnificence beyond compare."[11] Herod was king of a prosperous Israeli empire that produced annual revenues of more than $70 million, according to Josephus.

King Herod employed more than a thousand large wagons to transport the quarried limestone that was used in the construction of the enlarged Temple structure. While some of the foundation stones were taken from a quarry near the present-day Knesset (the Israeli parliament building), many of the large stones were carved from the Royal Caverns deep beneath the northeastern quarter of Jerusalem. Huge wagons transported the stones from the Royal Caverns through the subterranean entrance to the Temple Mount.[12]

The Roman historian Tacitus, who was a contemporary of the apostle Paul, wrote with great admiration of the glories of the Temple as it existed in the days of Herod the Great: "The temple resembled a citadel, and had its own walls, which were more laboriously constructed than the others. Even the colonnades with which it was surrounded formed an admirable outwork. It contained an inexhaustible spring; there were subterranean excavations in the hill, and tanks and cisterns for holding rain water."[13]

For all the glories of the rebuilt and enlarged Second Temple, it stood in Jerusalem for only eighty-seven years before the Roman legions laid utter waste to the city and Herod's Temple. The Jews have not had a Temple in Jerusalem during the intervening nineteen centuries. But based on recent developments in Israel, that could soon change.

■ ■ ■ ■

THREE:
RECOVERING LOST
TEMPLE TREASURES

PURSUING THE CLUES FOUND IN THE
COPPER SCROLL

■ ■ ■ ■

So was ended all the work
that king Solomon made
for the house of the LORD.
And Solomon brought in the things
which David his father had dedicated;
even the silver, and the gold, and the
     vessels,
did he put among the treasures
of the house of the LORD.

1 Kings 7:51

One of the most confusing mysteries to students of biblical studies and archaeology revolves around the question of what happened to the sacred, enormously costly treasures from both the First and Second Temples. During the final months of the Roman army's siege of the Second Temple in AD 70, two Jewish sects, the Essenes and the Zealots, vigorously defended the holy sanctuary. Numerous Jewish traditions and legends maintain that some of the sacred items were hidden during the siege to prevent the Roman army from looting the Temple treasury. The discovery of hidden tunnels beneath the Temple Mount shows that the priests and Temple guards had the means to hide the treasures and also to remove sacred objects for safekeeping away from the Temple Mount.

Clues Found in the Copper Scroll

After the Dead Sea Scrolls were discovered in a cave in 1947, scholars soon realized that the two-thousand-year-old Qumran manuscripts threw new light on events that occurred in the first century during the fall of Jerusalem. In March 1953 another curious scroll was discovered in Cave 3, near the ruins of the ancient village of Qumran on the west side of the Dead Sea. Out of thousands of manuscripts and portions of manuscripts discovered in the Dead Sea caves, all were written on parchment or leather, save one extraordinary scroll that was made of copper. The rolled-up scroll was composed of three copper sheets riveted together. It was approximately eight feet long and one foot wide. This metallic manuscript, officially named 3Q15 (based on the cave in which it was discovered), became known as the Copper Scroll.

The metal had deteriorated and corroded over two thousand years. However, after several years of careful restoration work, an archaeologist used a jeweler's saw to cut the tightly rolled scroll sideways, and the brittle metal was unrolled to allow access to the writing. The unknown author had used chisels to painstakingly engrave Hebrew letters into the copper sheets. The Copper

Scroll revealed a detailed list of sixty-four secret locations where the Jewish Essene priests had hidden gold and silver treasures from the Temple. The buried treasure mentioned on the list includes a number of sacred Temple vessels, manuscripts, gold and silver bullion, the oil of anointing, and the breastplate of the high priest.

The list is a basic accounting of sacred Temple treasures that were hidden away until they could be recovered for use in the future Temple. There is no embellishment or poetry in the text, such as you would expect to find if the list were an imaginary treasure story or symbolic myth. Further attesting to the accuracy of the list contained in the Copper Scroll, many of the descriptions match certain caves and cisterns surrounding Wadi Ha Keppah, near Qumran, by the shores of the Dead Sea. Ancient maps identify this area as the valley of Qumran, and locations can be identified with the help of a series of toponyms — place names that have definite meanings in the local language.

Among the sixty-four listed sites, three major areas are described in the Copper Scroll, including locations near Qumran, in southern Jerusalem centered on Mount Zion, and in an area on the east of the Jordan River in present-day Jordan. These locations are known to have been major centers of Essene settlement and activity.

As an example of an item included on the list, here is the translation done by archaeologist Dr. Bargil Pixner. This is the description for site fifty-four in the Copper Scroll: "Close by (BTKN ' SLM) on the treading place (BHBSH) at the top of the rock facing west against the garden of Sadok, under the great stone slab of the water outlet: untouchable (anathema!) (HRM)."[1] This particular item is obviously a very sacred object from the Temple. A special curse, "anathema," was proclaimed against anyone who might disturb its resting place.

Many details of the topographical descriptions are subject to interpretation. One problem is that a great deal of wind and occasional water erosion has transformed the smaller topographical features of the Qumran area. It's not easy to match the described landmarks to the present-day terrain, due to changes in the physical features of the land over the past two thousand years.

THE SEARCH FOR ADDITIONAL CLUES

In addition to the sixty-four sites listed in the Copper Scroll, researchers now believe there are many more sites where scrolls and other Temple treasures were hidden. The Qumran Essene community existed for more than two centuries until its destruction in AD 70 by the Romans, and they used hundreds of caves as hiding places for their manuscripts and other treasures. Many scholars believe there are additional Essene manuscripts that remain undiscovered.

A group of archaeologists is resuming the search for additional manuscripts and other artifacts in the Qumran area. In addition to traditional methods, researchers are using high-tech tools to locate buried treasures. A team from NASA developed technology that enables scientists to do a noninvasive molecular frequency analysis of subsurface features that lie hundreds of feet beneath a given target area. During the Apollo moon landings, for example, an earlier version of this technology enabled astronauts to determine which areas would most likely yield useful deep-core mineral samples. Noninvasive frequency analysis reads elements of the electromagnetic spectrum that indicate the type of molecules found in materials hidden far beneath the surface. Using this technology, archaeologists can locate underground caves, rooms, tunnels, and even objects within those spaces.

Use of this frequency analysis has already

shown that as many as forty clay jars may still be buried at Qumran. Further, the readings indicate that the jars are intact and may contain parchment manuscripts. More than thirty other readings picked up indications of another copper scroll, pottery, wood, various metals, and leather. Based on these readings and additional explorations, the Israeli government has issued written permission for the research group to commence a dig to recover these objects. If manuscripts are discovered, the Israeli government has said it will release the scrolls to the larger scholarly community for examination. It will take several years for archaeologists to dig down to the largest cave, forty feet below the surface, because they must follow exacting archaeological requirements and record the artifacts that are discovered at each layer.

HIDDEN TREASURE FROM THE TEMPLE

A number of Dead Sea Scroll archaeologists led by Prof. J. T. Milik, associated with the University of London, initially concluded that the Copper Scroll's list of hidden artifacts was nothing more than a fanciful tale of buried treasure. The basic reason many scholars rejected the list as an accounting of actual Second Temple treasures had to do with the enormous value of the treasures described. By the Copper Scroll's accounting, the hidden treasure amounted to some 3,282 talents of gold and 1,280 talents of silver. An ancient Hebrew talent varied from 75 pounds to 125 pounds, so equating a talent to approximately one hundred pounds of metal, at current prices the combined 4,500 talents of gold and silver would be valued at more than $2.5 billion.

However, if you consider that the Temple treasury was the repository not only for monetary gifts to the Temple and religious articles of value but also held Israel's national secular wealth, then the combined value of items mentioned on the list does not seem out of line. The Temple treasury contained an enormous amount of sacred gold and silver objects and also functioned as a central bank for the entire nation, both the government and private citizens.

The Roman writer Cicero complained that Israel had accumulated vast treasures from the enormous amounts of gold contributed every year by millions of faithful Jews throughout the Diaspora (the exiles who were scattered throughout the known world).[2] It is estimated that up to ten million Jews lived in exile east of Jerusalem in the area of present-day Syria, Jordan, Saudi Arabia, Afghanistan, Iraq, and Iran. An equal number of Jews lived in the western Roman Empire in Europe and North Africa. The Jewish historian Flavius Josephus wrote that when General Pompey captured Jerusalem in 63 BC, Crassus demanded and received an immediate tribute of "more than 10,000 talents" from the Temple treasury.[3]

A large portion of the annual Temple revenues was derived from the half shekel Temple tribute that was demanded annually from every male citizen of Israel, from the millions of religious Jews living outside Israel, and from a large number of proselytes (Gentiles who had embraced Judaism). The Temple half shekel, which was used solely for religious purposes, had twice the value of the regular shekel and was equal to two days' wages for a typical laborer. It is probable that the annual Temple tribute amounted to almost a billion dollars every year. The tribute accumulated each year and over the centuries produced an immense treasury.

The value of this treasury explains the elaborate measures that were taken to guard the Temple. In an unusual passage found in the book of Revelation, John wrote, "Blessed is he that watcheth, and keepeth his garments" (Revelation 16:15). This passage alludes to the requirement that any Temple guard who fell asleep while on sentry duty would have his clothing set on fire by the chief officer as a punishment for his negligence. (See the Jewish commentary Middoth 11:12, a part of the Mishneh.) Security was under the direction of the "captain of the temple," mentioned in Acts 4:1, who supervised the day and night guards and was in control of the key gates to the Temple and the various courts of worship. Guards served around the clock in twenty-four security positions. Jewish records suggest that 240 priests from the tribe of Levi, plus as many as 24 additional priests, served on security duty every night.

SACRED OBJECTS FROM THE TEMPLE

Beyond coins and religious objects made of silver and gold, the list of hidden artifacts includes ceremonial items that hold great significance for the rebuilding of the Temple and the resumption of Temple worship and sacrifice. A fascinating copper scroll was found in 1952 in Cave 8 at Qumran. This scroll, now in a museum in Amman, Jordan, confirms that the last offering of the sacrifice of the red heifer occurred in AD

68, just before the destruction of Jerusalem in AD 70. During the conflict, priests took the heifer's ashes from the Temple in a clay vessel and buried the vessel along with other sacred objects so they could be recovered in the last days. If the ashes from the red heifer were recovered, they could be used in the ritual cleansing of the Temple Mount and a rebuilt sanctuary. The ashes are needed to create the "water of purification" (see Numbers 19) that will be used to purify the priests, the sacred worship vessels, and the Third Temple.

A portion of this scroll reads: "On the way from Jericho to Succukah, by the River ha Kippa, in the tomb of Zadok, the priest, which is a cave that has two openings. On the opening on the side by the north, the view toward the east, dig two and one-half cubits under the plaster and there will be found the Kalal [a vessel made with clay and dung from the red heifer, which holds the ashes of the last sacrificed red heifer] and under it one scroll."[4] Naturally, it is difficult to match this description with a current location, but several investigations are being conducted under the auspices of the chief rabbi and the Israeli museums. Some Christian and Jewish students of prophecy believe that the ashes of the red

heifer will be recovered before the rebuilding of the Temple. I am aware of several
archaeological investigations in Israel that
seek additional information about the ashes
and also the ark of the covenant. Recovering these sacred artifacts is key to rebuilding the Temple.

There is a curious tradition mentioned in
the Talmud that Gentiles will assist the Jews
in the recovery of Temple implements. This
is the reason the Jewish leadership has been
willing to accept help from interested
Gentiles. One archaeological group has
been searching in a cave south of Jericho
for the ashes of the red heifer and for additional scrolls that would describe the locations of lost Temple vessels.

THE DISCOVERY OF THE OIL OF ANOINTING

Using information found in the Copper
Scroll, an archaeological team, which included one of my friends, launched a search
to recover the sacred oil of anointing, which
had been lost since the first century. The
team searched Cave 11 in Qumran and
found a clay vessel approximately five inches
high that contained oil that had solidified as
a gelatin-like substance, somewhat like
molasses. The clay jar had been wrapped in
palm leaves and was buried three feet deep

81

in a pit, which helped protect the oil from the extreme high temperatures in the Dead Sea caves. The oil in the jar was an unusual incense oil, and it was possible that the oil contained the five ingredients the Bible requires for the oil for anointing Israel's kings. The same oil also was used as the fragrance on the oblation to create a sweet-smelling savor.

This sacred oil of anointing, known as the *shemen afarsimon,* originated during the Exodus. God commanded Moses to create the oil of anointing using five ingredients:

Take thou also unto thee principal spices, of pure myrrh five hundred shekels, and of sweet cinnamon half so much, even two hundred and fifty shekels, and of sweet calamus two hundred and fifty shekels, and of cassia five hundred shekels, after the shekel of the sanctuary, and of oil olive an hin: and thou shalt make it an oil of holy ointment, an ointment compound after the art of the apothecary: it shall be an holy anointing oil. And thou shalt anoint the tabernacle of the congregation therewith, and the ark of the testimony. . . . And thou shalt anoint Aaron and his sons, and consecrate them, that they may minister unto me in the priest's office. And thou shalt speak unto the children of Israel, saying, This shall be an holy anointing oil unto me throughout your generations. (Exodus 30:23–26, 30–31)

When the oil that was discovered in Cave 11 was analyzed, it was shown to be composed of five ingredients, exactly as God had commanded Moses. Carbon-14 radioactive dating indicated that the oil is almost two thousand years old, from the time of the Second Temple. The Talmud declares that a drop of this special oil will cause water to turn milky white. It is alleged that this oil did in fact turn water milky white. The Israel Museum verified that the composition of the oil is unlike that of any other oil they have evaluated. Intensive testing by the Pharmaceutical Department of Hebrew University established that the oil inside the clay vessel was the ancient oil of anointing. It was given to the two chief rabbis of Israel for safekeeping.

One of the five ingredients in this oil is the rare persimmon or balsam (afarsimon) oil, which was so valued by the Egyptian queen Cleopatra that she asked her lover, the Roman general Mark Antony, to give her a grove of balsam trees in a wadi near Jericho. In fact, there were only two groves in the whole of the Middle East where the precious balsam trees grew — one in Jericho and another in a wadi near En Gedi on the west side of the Dead Sea.

When it became apparent that the Romans were going to destroy Jerusalem and the Temple, priests burned the two groves of balsam trees to keep them out of the hands of the Romans. However, with the destruction of the only two existing balsam groves, it became impossible to reconstitute the ancient oil of anointing. Some Jewish scholars argued that the inability to create the legitimate oil of anointing would prevent the Jews from ever resuming legitimate Temple worship. Without the oil of anointing, it would seem to be impossible to anoint the sacred objects and the priests. However, the discovery of this ancient sample of the oil of anointing makes it possible to anoint the Temple, the sacred vessels, the Cohanim (priests descended directly from the sons of Aaron), and the Messiah-King of Israel.

I believe the discovery of the ancient oil of anointing will prove to be a key event in setting the stage for the fulfillment of the prophecies in the last days. With the anointing oil now in the possession of Israel's chief rabbis, the Temple can be rebuilt, and

Temple worship can be reinstituted. The Third Temple, the ark of the covenant, the table of shewbread, the menorah, the incense altar, the altar of burnt offering, and the Cohanim will be anointed with this sacred oil. Jesus will finally be anointed as Israel's Messiah by the high priest, using the consecrated oil of anointing, when He returns in glory to save Jerusalem from the armies of the Antichrist. Jesus will cleanse the Third Temple and establish His kingdom forever.

When the Lord returns, the oil of anointing will be used to usher in His messianic rule.

CLUES FOUND IN THE EZEKIEL TABLETS

In addition to the Copper Scroll, there is a second ancient record — known as the Ezekiel Tablets — that sheds light on other treasures missing from the Temple. There is a theory that stone tablets containing the text of the book of Ezekiel were buried in the tomb of the prophet, which still exists in Iraq. In support of this possibility, the Talmud describes the ancient Jewish custom of burying manuscripts with the bodies of their sages and scholars.[5] During an examination of several passages in the Talmud, I came across curious references to the tomb of the prophet Ezekiel. It is described as a double tomb designed to hold two bodies, similar to the tomb of Abraham and Sarah in Hebron, Israel. The Talmud recounts that a Persian caliph, an ancient prince of Babylon, visited the tomb of Ezekiel. When Persian officials entered the tomb, they were surprised to discover the remains of a body lying on marble tablets.

This mention in an ancient text of marble tablets within the tomb of Ezekiel is tantalizing. Could they be the same tablets that Bedouin Arabs claimed they took from the tomb of Ezekiel early in the nineteenth century? While this account does not prove that the Ezekiel Tablets originated in the ancient tomb of Ezekiel, it certainly provides some historical evidence in favor of that argument.

There is another fascinating historical footnote connected to the tomb of Ezekiel. Louis Ginzberg's book *The Legends of the Jews* describes an attempt by robbers to break into the same tomb in a vain attempt "to take some books from the grave of Ezekiel."[6] Again, the legend reveals that the attempt to steal the "books" was unsuccessful. The word translated "books" could refer either to scrolls or tablets, since the ancient Jews did not use bound books. This reference supports the traditional Arab account that marble tablets were taken from Ezekiel's tomb at a much later date.

In 1952 a close friend of Yitzhak Ben-Zvi, the second president of Israel, was allowed to view the mysterious Ezekiel Tablets, which contain the major portion of the inspired biblical text of Ezekiel. Aside from the unique nature of biblical text engraved on marble tablets, the text is in bas-relief. *Bas-relief* means that the craftsman carefully carved away the background to allow the raised Hebrew letters to be easily read. This incredibly costly and time-consuming process proclaimed the importance of Ezekiel's inspired text, and it created an impossible task for anyone who might desire to amend or alter God's inspired revelation.[7] After examining these fascinating stones, Ben-Zvi's friend turned to the president and said, "You know, I believe that I have seen a picture of one or two of these stones several years ago." Unfortunately, the man couldn't remember which book or journal contained the photo. As far as President Yitzhak Ben-Zvi knew, no one had ever been allowed to publish photos of the Ezekiel Tablets. This raised an interesting question: if a photo of one or two of the tablets had in fact been published, was it possible it had been a picture of tablets that were missing from the collection? Years of diligent research failed to turn up the missing photo.

One day in a dark corner of a special library in Jerusalem, I was completing research on the Copper Scroll. After hours of following one false lead after another, I finally tracked down an elusive reference to the Copper Scroll in an enormous group of documents and volumes that covered an entire wall of the library. I opened a French text, *Revue Biblique,* to an article that dealt with the Copper Scroll. To my great surprise, at the end of the article the author, J. T. Milik, a leading Dead Sea Scroll scholar, included a photo of one of the marble tablets. He had a partial description of the unusual text and described how he had located it. Father Jean Starcky, another famous Dead Sea Scroll scholar, shot the photograph. Curiously, the photos of the marble tablet and the written description were not listed in either the journal's index or its table of contents.

The photo revealed a marble tablet with text in ancient Hebrew script in bas-relief, precisely like the Ezekiel Tablets. However, the mysterious text in the photo did not contain any part of the text of the book of

Ezekiel. Rather, it contained a history of the treasures lost six centuries earlier from Solomon's Temple (586 BC) and the secret hiding places of those treasures, said to be near Mount Carmel in northern Israel.

The journal article states: "The copper scroll originating in Cave 3 of Qumran has a catalog of treasures. . . . Another writing is most interesting because it relates in detail the treasures of the Temple of Jerusalem hidden about the time of the destruction by the Babylonians. It was printed in 1853 by A. Jellinek in *Bet-ha-Midrash II,* Leipzig, pages 26 and 85–91. A duplicate of this 'Treatise of the Sacred Vessels' is to be read on the 'Plates (Tablets) of Beirut.' "[8] Prudence forces me to refrain from providing the topographical details of the secret sites the priests used to hide these treasures from Solomon's Temple.

Milik also reveals the story behind the photo of the intriguing tablet. Years earlier he had discovered several marble slabs engraved with letters in bas-relief in the basement of a house in Beirut. They were destined for a synagogue in Syria or Lebanon. The vast majority of the tablets contained the entire text of Ezekiel, but on the last two slabs were found inscribed the history of Temple treasures hidden near Mount

Carmel and the descriptions of their hiding places.[9]

At some time in the late 1940s, Milik had seen the Ezekiel Tablets in Beirut. Now, after all these years, the tablets have turned up in Jerusalem. Hopefully, scholars will be able to determine their true source and their correct dating. It is my hope that further research, based on the text of the two tablets that Milik described, will lead to the discovery of the items that have been missing from Solomon's Temple for more than 2,500 years.

■ ■ ■ ■

FOUR:
EXPLORING THE
ANCIENT CITY
UNDERNEATH
JERUSALEM

FASCINATING DISCOVERIES IN THE
SUBTERRANEAN CITY

■ ■ ■ ■

Take heed now;
for the LORD hath chosen thee
to build an house for the sanctuary:
be strong, and do it.
Then David gave to Solomon his son
the pattern of the porch, and of the houses
    thereof,
and of the treasuries thereof.

1 Chronicles 28:10–11

For three thousand years, Jewish citizens, pagan invaders, and Jewish and Christian pilgrims have walked the stone streets of Jerusalem filled with a sense of wonder. The magnificent buildings and huge defensive walls inspire awe in all who see them. But despite the fact that tens of thousands of books have been written about this fascinating city, few visitors are aware of the secret city that lies far beneath the Temple Mount and Jerusalem's Old City. This underground city was constructed over many centuries to be used to hide Temple treasures and to protect the citizens of Jerusalem during times of invasion.

Jerusalem has been invaded at least twenty-seven times, more than any other city in history. The list of major invaders includes Egypt, Assyria, Babylon, Syria, Greece, Rome, Persia, the Muslims, the Crusaders, the Ottoman Turks, Britain, and finally the Jewish soldiers of the modern State of Israel during the Six-Day War in 1967. Despite these invasions and occupations, most of the secret tunnels, treasuries, food storage chambers, cisterns, and underground shelters have remained unknown. This enormous subterranean infrastructure has served the needs of kings and rebels, priests and besieged citizens during periods of peace and times of war.

CONSTRUCTION OF THE UNDERGROUND CITY

In 1000 BC the Temple Mount plateau, which covers an area of thirty-five acres, was artificially leveled and then enlarged by the construction of gigantic substructures according to the command of King Solomon, in accordance with the precise plans of God that were given to Solomon's father, King David.[1]

The existence of the underground city was kept secret over many centuries because the caverns served the political and religious purposes of the leadership of Israel and the city of Jerusalem. As just one example, a tunnel referred to in the book of Jeremiah was discovered in 1990. This amazing tunnel leads under the Old City from Jeremiah's prison to the Temple. Jeremiah 39:4

This photograph, c. 1900, shows a portion of the network of tunnels that run underneath the Temple Mount.

reveals that as the city finally surrendered to the Babylonian army, King Zedekiah and his soldiers "fled, and went forth out of the city by night, by the way of the king's garden, by the gate betwixt the two walls:

and he went out the way of the plain."

Researchers and archaeologists have come across the remains of numerous tunnels, rooms, treasuries, and cisterns in many areas of the Old City. But few have guessed that the *entire* city of Jerusalem sits above a honeycomb of underground passageways. I have visited the underground city on many of my research trips. I have studied hundreds of Jewish, Muslim, and Christian manuscripts that discuss portions of the subterranean structures. And I have interviewed men who have devoted their lives to unlocking the secrets of this mysterious subterranean city. After almost three decades of reading musty old books from rabbis and early Christian explorers, as well as exploring the tunnel system myself, I am convinced that we still probably know less than 10 percent of the secrets of underground Jerusalem and the Temple Mount (see photograph).

The writings of the Jewish sages, including the Talmud and Moses Maimonides' *Mishneh Torah,* refer to the construction and use of this underground complex at various times during Jerusalem's history. According to Mishneh Meilah 3, 3 and Succah 53a, King David was the first to dig into the bedrock of Mount Moriah, north of the city of David, so he could lay out the foundation lines of the future Temple (see 1 Chronicles 28:11–12). David's early work was followed by the skilled architects of his son King Solomon.

The extraordinary amounts of water needed in the Temple for purification and drainage purposes required the creation of a vast water tunnel system. The need for storage chambers led to the construction of an interconnected system of guardrooms, holding chambers for sacrificial animals, and prison cells. While the area near the sanctuary was considered holy, the areas farther away on the Temple Mount were used for fortifications, espionage, and communication needs.

Maimonides explored the Temple Mount in AD 1165. Although most rabbis today believe that no Jews should enter any part of the Temple Mount lest they inadvertently defile the Holy of Holies, the great Maimonides declared, "On Thursday, 5th Marcheshvan 4926 [AD 1165] I entered the great and Holy House and prayed there."[2] Rabbi Eliezer Azikri recorded this in his book *Sefer Charedim,* copying it from Maimonides' own handwriting. The reason Maimonides would have entered the Temple courtyard with such confidence is that because of his lifelong study and personal observations, he knew precisely where the site of the Holy of Holies was located.

In the *Mishneh Torah* volume *The Laws of God's Chosen House,* based on detailed eyewitness accounts from the time of the Second Temple, Maimonides states: "Mount Moriah, the Temple Mount, measured 500 cubits by 500 cubits. It was surrounded by a wall. The earth beneath was hollowed out to prevent contracting [ritual impurity] due to *Tumas Ohel.* Arches above arches were built underneath [for support]. It was entirely covered, one colonnade inside another."[3]

Jewish commentators claim that the prohibitions against touching a dead body were extended to protect the Temple Mount against spiritual defilement. Because death is directly connected to the curse and punishment of sin, the touching of anything dead would ritually defile a priest or worshiper and prevent him from participating in Temple worship services (see Numbers 19). Even a corpse buried in the earth below the Temple would render the sacrifices spiritually invalid, according to the rabbis. According to Parah, chapter 3, Mishneh 3, "The entire earth below was hollowed out . . . to prevent the possibility of impurity from a grave under the Temple courtyard." According to Jewish law and tradition, no sepulchers for bodies were allowed within Jerusalem except those of the House of King David and the prophetess Huldah.[4]

This ritual defilement was known as tumas ohel, and the sages believed the creation of an open space by building an elaborate series of arches erected over arches below the pavement of the Temple surface spiritually insulated the top of the Temple Mount from the tumas. Defilement was always assumed to exist in the earth underneath an ancient and often-besieged city. The ground underneath Jerusalem would contain the remains of soldiers killed in battle, for instance. In light of the assumed spiritual defilement, much of the ground underneath the Temple Mount was hollowed out. This elaborate subterranean structure contained numerous rooms that were used as treasuries, guardrooms, water cisterns, and storage rooms that contemporary Jewish historians estimate would have held enough grain reserves to feed the population of Jerusalem during a siege lasting more than a dozen years.

My own explorations have focused on Mount Zion, the Western Wall excavations, the Old City, and Golgotha, plus extensive research on the early explorations carried out by English, French, and German explorers and pioneer archaeologists with the Palestine Exploration Fund beginning in 1860. It appears that the subterranean passages connect in a vast system of tunnels extending from the Pool of Siloam area in the south of the ancient city of David all the way to Golgotha — Calvary — to the north of the city walls and the Gate of Damascus. A section of the tunnel system connects westward to the Upper City (now the Jewish Quarter) and underlies portions of the Muslim and Armenian Quarters of the Old City. The area of the Old City of Jerusalem (within the walls) is approximately three hundred acres, and the subterranean structures exist under a substantial portion of the city.

When people first hear about the vast underground city, their first question often is "How could such a city be carved out of solid rock in ancient times?" Much of the answer involves the unusual nature of the limestone that forms the foundation of the city of Jerusalem. When I was in one cave beneath the city, a small stone broke off from the ceiling overhead. As I reached up to touch the limestone that had just been exposed, I was surprised to feel how soft the rock surface was. I could carve a small square in the limestone with a fingernail. The archaeologist with me explained that while the limestone is very easily worked when it's first exposed to air, in a few years the stone surface becomes as hard as any other stone. This explains how workers in ancient times could relatively easily carve tunnels through the limestone with basic iron chisels and picks, and after they had dug a tunnel, the air would harden the rock's surface over time. Thus, the limestone of Jerusalem was ideal for the construction of massive underground structures.

Some of the large caverns under the city are natural, but most were carved out to create chambers for storage and other uses. The Mishneh tells us that passageways allowed priests who became ritually defiled during Temple service to exit secretly from underneath the Temple Mount. One of these tunnels leads to a secret gate of the Levites that opened through the underground portions of the subterranean Western Wall. This special gate was described in the Mishneh as existing to the side of a larger gate, a massive gate that took six men to close. If a Levite priest was delayed after the main gate was locked, he had to use the special Gate of the Levites. This small gate measured only thirty inches wide by fifty inches high and required a person to stoop to pass through it. The discovery of this gate has helped researchers determine the original location of the ancient Temple.

Several of the tunnels underneath the Temple Mount lead directly to *mikvehs* (ritual baths), which the priests used to cleanse themselves before entering the Temple. One of the most interesting mikvehs, discovered in the excavation of the Western Wall tunnel, was located just outside the northern portion of the wall at the King's Gate, which is now sealed. This gate originally allowed the king to exit from the Tower of Antonia (the palace) and privately prepare himself to enter the Temple. Additionally, there were tunnels that allowed the high priest and others to privately enter and exit the Temple to wash at their personal mikvehs without risk of defilement by contact with spiritually unclean people or objects.

Maimonides described these tunnels being accessed through "winding underground passageways," which is a good description of one of the tunnels my wife, Kaye, and I explored.[5] Priests who had ritually defiled themselves could use the tunnels to leave the Temple through the northern Taddi Gate of the Temple Mount.[6]

The Mishneh, Middoth 1.6 describes a secret chamber that was hollowed out under the Chamber of Shewbread beneath the Temple itself. This chamber was used as a repository for the stones of the ancient altar. The altar stones had been desecrated by Antiochus Epiphanes, the Syrian tyrant, in 168 BC through the sacrifice of a pig on the altar of the Temple. When the Jewish Hasmonean priests cleansed the Temple three years later on Hanukkah (the 25th of Chisleu) in 165 BC, they were not sure what they should do with the defiled stones. They carved out the secret chamber and stored the altar stones there "until the Messiah should come and instruct them in what should be done" with them.[7]

There is a curious story recorded in a Jewish commentary that states that a magician by the name of Parvah dug a secret tunnel through the limestone under the Temple so he could come up inside the inner courtyard. He planned to clandestinely witness the high priest in the secret Temple worship. This passage declares that Parvah was killed for defiling the secret precincts. Interestingly, the Chamber of Parvah in the Second Temple was named after the magician to remind others of the sanctity of the Lord's House.[8]

TEMPLE TREASURES HIDDEN IN THE UNDERGROUND CITY

There is reason to believe that treasures from the Temple and other sacred items have been hidden underneath Jerusalem for millenniums. Some Jewish sages declare that King Josiah was given special prophetic insight of the coming destruction of the sanctuary by the Babylonians — some thirty-five years before the burning of the Temple in 586 BC. Accordingly, they believe that God led the king and the priests to bury the treasures of the Temple, including the oil of anointing, the rod of Aaron, and the pot of manna. It is said that these items were hidden in a special chamber created for this purpose some four hundred years earlier by King Solomon.[9] Additionally, the Talmud states that the ark of the covenant (or its replica) was hidden in the same underground chamber.

Maimonides recounted the belief of the ancient sages: "When Solomon built the

Temple, he was aware that it would ultimately be destroyed. He constructed a chamber in which the ark could be entombed below the Temple in deep, maze like vaults. King Josiah commanded that the ark be entombed in the chamber built by Solomon, as it is said (2 Chronicles 35:3) 'And he said to the Levites who were enlightened above all of Israel. Place the Holy Ark in the chamber built by Solomon, the son of David, King of Israel. You will no longer carry it on your shoulders. Now; serve the Lord, your God.' When it was entombed, Aaron's staff, the vial of manna, and the oil used for anointing were entombed with it. All these sacred articles did not return in the Second Temple."[10]

In Exodus 16:33 Moses commanded Aaron to "take a pot, and put an omer full [one gallon] of manna therein, and lay it up before the LORD, to be kept for your generations." Also Numbers 17:9–10 records that following the revolt of Korah, when the leadership of the subtribe of Korah contested who would have the key role of the priesthood of Israel, God commanded Moses to "bring Aaron's rod" within the ark of the covenant as a proof that the Lord had chosen the Aaronic priesthood.

When my wife, Kaye, and I were in the

Western Wall excavation tunnels exactly opposite the original Temple location, we noticed a picture of a menorah (the seven-branched candelabrum) hanging from a spike. I asked the Jewish archaeologist who accompanied us why the religious picture was hanging in a working archaeological dig. He explained that, as nearly as they could calculate, the ancient menorah in the Second Temple stood in a line to the east of where we were standing — directly behind that picture through the Western Wall. He also said something quite curious that I understood later, after studying Maimonides' "censored" volume on the Temple. He said, "Grant, we believe that the sacred ark of the covenant is located in a secret chamber directly to the east behind this Western Wall." At the time we were standing in a tunnel that is more than one hundred feet below the level where you would walk if you visited the Temple Mount today. The archaeologist had calculated the possible location of the Temple treasures hidden by King Josiah, in the chamber created by Solomon, one hundred feet below the floor of the First Temple.

But could King Josiah really have hidden the ark of the covenant? My research indicates that the ark disappeared from Israel long before Josiah's reign. I believe the burden of evidence suggests that the ark was removed to Ethiopia near the conclusion of the reign of Prince Menelik, King Solomon's son with the queen of Sheba. The Ethiopian Royal Chronicles affirmed that at that time a perfect replica of the ark was created by Solomon's craftsmen. The Ethiopian history claims that the replica of the ark was substituted for the real ark in the Holy of Holies. If this tradition is accurate, then King Josiah might have hidden the replica in the secret underground chamber.

The *Jerusalem Talmud* refers to the existence of a second ark, created by Temple craftsmen. It states: "A second Ark containing the Tablets broken by Moses accompanied the people to war at all times."[11] While this does not prove that a replica of the ark was made, it certainly adds evidence to the Ethiopian Royal Chronicle's tradition of the creation of a duplicate of the ark in the days of Solomon. Due to the nature of the design and materials of the ark of the covenant, a perfect replica would be virtually impossible to distinguish from the original. It was covered by gold that does not deteriorate or tarnish and would appear identical to any observer. Only further research will conclusively prove the true location of the lost ark.

However, the prophecies of the Bible strongly suggest that the lost ark (wherever the Lord has preserved it) will play a major role in inspiring the Jews to build the Third Temple. (For more on the ark of the covenant, see chapter 8.)

THE UNDERGROUND STRUCTURES AND PASSAGES

Beyond the ritual baths, the huge cisterns for water storage, and rooms for hiding Temple treasures, underground space was needed to hold the enormous quantity of animals used in the daily sacrifices. Consider that 1 Kings 8 tells us that on the first day of the dedication of the First Temple, Solomon sacrificed 120,000 sheep. You can understand the need for a sophisticated livestock control system beneath the Temple Mount, involving ramps and holding pens. In addition, chambers were needed to dispose of the sacrificed animals, both the meat that was kept for use by the Levites and the parts that were disposed of. In *Wars of the Jews,* Josephus recorded that during the last Passover before the Romans besieged Jerusalem, the priests sacrificed 256,000 sheep in the afternoon of the Passover. With one sheep required to be sacrificed for each family or small related group, this number of animals is consistent with Josephus's estimate of a temporary two-million-person population during the feast.

Additionally, there were large underground chambers that served as guardrooms for the treasury of the Temple (see 1 Chronicles 28:11–12). King Hezekiah violated the security rules in place since the reign of David and boastfully revealed the riches of the Temple to the pagan ambassadors of the rising Babylonian Empire. When Isaiah asked Hezekiah what had he revealed to the ambassadors, he replied: "All that is in mine house have they seen: there is nothing among my treasures that I have not shewed them" (Isaiah 39:4). The prophet replied: "Behold, the days come, that all that is in thine house, and that which thy fathers have laid up in store until this day, shall be carried to Babylon: nothing shall be left, saith the LORD" (Isaiah 39:6). As Isaiah prophesied, years later reports of Israel's stupendous wealth attracted the unwelcome interest of Babylonian king Nebuchadnezzar. He came with a mighty army in 605 BC, again in 597 BC, and finally in 586 BC to destroy the Temple and to carry off the wealth that God had allowed

Israel to accumulate.

When King Herod rebuilt and enlarged the Second Temple, he was very much concerned with the possibility of a revolt against his rule. Because he was an Idumaean and not a true Israelite, he owed his rule to the favor of hated Rome. He built a number of fortresses, including Herodium and the mountain fortress of Masada, to provide places of impregnable refuge in the case of revolution. Additionally, Herod had his engineers build a secret escape tunnel that led diagonally from his palace north of the Temple sanctuary, underneath the Temple to a special defense tower near the Eastern Gate.[12]

A few years ago several knowledgeable Israeli friends who love archaeology revealed an astonishing discovery that has not yet been publicized. After we discussed King Herod's escape tunnel, my friend said, "And he didn't stop there [the Eastern Gate]." He explained that a few years ago he and a few others had discovered that a very narrow, eleven-mile-long escape tunnel provided a way of safety for the king that led from the Temple Mount across the Kidron Valley, past the Mount of Olives, and east toward King Herod's castle in the city of Jericho. The tunnel would allow only one person at a time to pass. Naturally, after two thousand years the passage is now mostly filled with silt and debris. We can scarcely imagine the years of backbreaking work required to construct this tunnel of refuge for the hated King Herod (see diagram).

A Tunnel Through Time into Biblical History

One of the most fascinating of the discoveries beneath the Temple Mount involved the opening of another secret tunnel system that was used as an escape route by the kings of Israel, including King Zedekiah during the siege by Babylon in 586 BC. In 1990, at the end of a visit to Israel, Kaye and I received a most unusual invitation. A telephone call from a rabbi who was deeply involved with Temple archaeological research asked if I would be interested in exploring even deeper underneath the Temple Mount. Of course I said yes. So Kaye and I met our Israeli friend at the Western Wall at 2:00 a.m. To our surprise, despite the drizzling rain, more than two dozen Jewish seminary students were dancing and worshiping at the Western Wall with their rabbi. My friend told me that since the capture of the Temple

111

Mount and the Western Wall in June 1967, the Western Wall is never left without worshipers, even through the long, cold nights of winter.

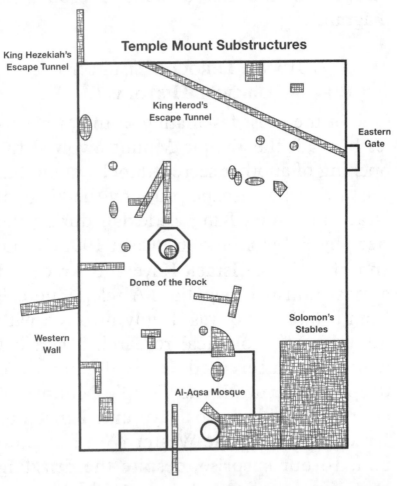

Temple Mount Substructures

King Hezekiah's Escape Tunnel

King Herod's Escape Tunnel

Eastern Gate

Dome of the Rock

Solomon's Stables

Western Wall

Al-Aqsa Mosque

This diagram shows the location of two ancient tunnels that run beneath the Temple Mount — escape tunnels put in place by King Hezekiah and King Herod.

As we began our explorations, we were able to visit and photograph many of the subterranean gates, tunnels, and rooms that we had not been able to photograph previously. As it was the middle of the night, there were almost no archaeologists or guards to interfere with our research. For two and a half hours, Kaye and I were thrilled to walk where few people in history have had the privilege of going. The floor was uneven and wet where rubble had been removed. The tunnels were so narrow in places that we had to turn and pass through walking sideways. Tunnel after tunnel opened into special guardrooms and ancient synagogues and storage chambers. After walking the entire length (more than 1,150 feet) of the Western Wall tunnel excavation, we arrived at a point under the foundations of the ancient Tower of Antonia, to the northwest of the Temple, where the kings of Israel built their palaces.

In the north end of the Western Wall tunnel, which parallels the Western Wall underneath one hundred fifty feet of rubble and the basements of Arab buildings, we came upon an unusual stone gate that cut through the enormous foundation stones of the Tower of Antonia and led up into the kings' palace. However, this huge gate, known as the King's Gate, had been sealed by large stones that were carefully fitted into the opening. Just opposite the gate, we found the remains of a large and elaborate mikveh, a ritual immersion bath, situated there for the use of the king to ritually purify himself prior to entering the Temple.

Passing this mikveh, which had been used by many of the kings of the Bible, we opened a steel gate that sealed off a newly opened tunnel complex that led to the north of the Temple Mount. When I asked for more information, we were told there was some mystery connected with it. Naturally that only whetted my appetite. (From my earliest years I have loved exploring tunnels and caverns. As a teenager I explored the huge cavern systems that ran underneath our family's resort camp west of Ottawa, Canada.) For the next two hours we followed the most amazing tunnel system for more than a mile and a half, with walls rising as high as sixty feet. What an experience. Now we truly were walking on stones that Israel's kings and prophets had trod.

The Bible records that when the Babylonian army besieged Jerusalem, Jeremiah warned King Zedekiah to surrender to Babylon because God had transferred the sovereignty of the world from Israel to the

Gentile empires (beginning the "times of the Gentiles" [Luke 21:24]). However, the wicked king ignored the explicit warning of God and locked Jeremiah in a prison that was fashioned out of a cistern located north of the Gate of Damascus, very near Golgotha. (The cistern is known today as the Grotto of Jeremiah.) The Scriptures record that when the Babylonian army finally broke through the walls of Jerusalem, Zedekiah decided to flee the city with his soldiers and family (see Jeremiah 39:4). Of course, he could not flee in secret with army staff officers and family members through a city that was under siege unless he had a hidden escape tunnel. Now, after twenty-five centuries, the proof supporting this biblical account has been revealed by the spade of the archaeologist. The tunnel that Kaye and I were exploring was the same tunnel used by King Zedekiah.

This tunnel is most unusual in that it is more than sixty feet high for much of its length. Yet the tunnel is only four to eight feet wide. The scriptural description "between the two walls" (see Jeremiah 52:7) is the most accurate that I could imagine to describe this remarkable escape tunnel, which led thousands of feet from the Temple Mount northward to emerge outside the walls of the city.

Jeremiah 52:7–11 and 2 Kings 25:4–7 record that the king, once he was outside the besieged city, was captured by the Babylonians, his children were killed before him, and then his eyes were blinded — exactly as Ezekiel had foretold (see Ezekiel 12:12–13). This came about because Zedekiah would not obey the command of God to submit to Babylon.

THE FIRST PHOTOS EVER TAKEN OF SOLOMON'S STABLES

In my personal library are hundreds of volumes by pilgrims, warriors, researchers, and archaeologists who have explored the Temple Mount. Under Turkish Muslim rule, it was forbidden for non-Muslims ("infidels") to enter and thereby defile the sanctity of the Temple Mount and especially the Dome of the Rock shrine or the Al-Aqsa Mosque. It became legal for non-Muslims to visit the sanctuary only in 1856. Before that, many explorers took grave, personal risks to penetrate the Temple Mount, using friendships and, occasionally, large gifts (baksheesh) to open the door. For several years I tried numerous times without success to arrange permission from the Waqf (the Muslim council that exercises administrative control of the Temple Mount) to enter the southwestern subterranean portion of the Temple Mount, an area known as Solomon's Stables.

In 1991 we were finally granted permission to explore this structure, which had not been visited by a Westerner since the 1850s, except for Moshe Dayan, Israel's minister of defense, following the Six-Day War in 1967. In all my research I have never seen published photographs of this mysterious building that give a sense of the huge subterranean construction Solomon used for the foundations for his Temple. We were able to photograph the rows of ancient columns that support the roof of Solomon's Stables. While the Crusaders used the stables for their horses (hay mangers and holes in the columns to tie the reins are evident), the building was used by King Solomon to hold some of his vast treasures.

The substructure extends 319 feet in an east-west direction toward the Western Wall and as much as 247 feet north from the southern wall of the Temple Mount. The stone floor gradually rises as one moves in a northerly direction, and it is easy to see how this ramplike effect would facilitate the movement of large numbers of oxen and sheep during major sacrifices.

I discovered evidence that centuries ago someone — possibly Crusaders, who used the Temple Mount as their headquarters in the eleventh and twelfth centuries — had completed some serious excavations in search of Temple treasures. Sadly, in the last ten years the Waqf authorities have destroyed the archaeological remnants of Solomon's Stables. The Waqf brought in bulldozers and massive stone saws to gut the ancient building to create the area's largest underground mosque. Tragically, their construction efforts destroyed artifacts that would have revealed much about the history of the Temple Mount. The Waqf ordered the hundreds of tons of debris to be dumped in the nearby Kidron Valley. Despite the fact that this wholesale destruction of perhaps the world's most important archaeological site was in complete violation of Israeli law, the Jewish authorities did nothing to stop the destruction. Just before the Waqf destroyed the site, I was able to go back to Solomon's Stables with a television crew. Thus we obtained the only known television footage of one of the most mysterious subterranean treasures from ancient times.

An Ancient Church Found Underground, Adjoining the Temple Mount

Among the remarkable archaeological treasures discovered underneath Jerusalem, perhaps the most unexpected is an ancient church. When Kaye and I were exploring the Western Wall tunnel excavation, we came upon an immense subterranean room located directly west of and opposite the Dome of the Rock and underneath the rubble of the Second Temple. Roman soldiers threw the stones of the destroyed Temple into this area, which was a large valley in the days of Christ.

After the destruction of Jerusalem in AD 70, the surviving inhabitants slowly began to rebuild some of the buildings. Naturally, they used the stones that were available, even though many of the edges and corners had been broken. As Kaye and I walked through the tunnels with our Israeli friend Yishai, we entered a colossal room, larger than any room we had yet explored. It was more than one hundred feet long and at one point fifty feet wide. The majestic roof arched some sixty feet above our heads. Built initially in the second century, this unexpected structure had been rebuilt during the time of the Crusades. The sixty-foot ceiling was many feet below the basements of the centuries-old Arab buildings just to the west of the Temple Mount.

The original structure was clearly formed in the shape of a cross, with the wings of the cross extending more than eighty feet across. The walls were obviously built with the original stones from the Second Temple. These stones were visible from the floor to about twelve feet in height. Thereafter the builders were forced to use newer and smaller stones to complete the structure. I asked my Israeli friend if this could be a Christian church located almost at the foot of the Western Wall. He slowly nodded yes. There are no Muslim or Jewish buildings in the world constructed in the shape of a cross. However, many early Roman Christian churches used this cross-shaped plan.

The location of this ancient church was unknown, except in legend, for more than a thousand years. To say that Israeli authorities were surprised to find a cross-shaped church built with the sacred stones of the Temple and located within one hundred feet of the Western Wall would be an understatement. Some of the archaeologists I talked to refused to admit openly that this structure could be a church. However, it could not be a Jewish or Muslim structure.

The implications are fascinating. Even after the destruction of Jerusalem, some of the Jews (including Messianic Jews) remained in the area until AD 135, when they were expelled by Emperor Hadrian. Does the existence of this church, built on this sacred location and using the sacred stones, imply that a large number of Jews became early Christian believers in the Messiah Jesus? It is hard to see how this church could have been built so close to the most sacred of Jewish sites, the Western Wall, unless a significant number of Jews had become believers in Jesus as the Messiah.

There are many more mysteries to be solved in future explorations underneath the city of Jerusalem. I fully expect that in the peaceful years of the coming Millennium, we will discover numerous new chambers and tunnels that will enlarge our understanding of the fascinating biblical and secular history of this most remarkable city.

We are living in prophetic times. Our generation has witnessed more specific prophecies fulfilled than any other generation in history. The rebirth of Israel after two thousand years of exile is an unprecedented miracle. The Lord has not only brought His people back to their Promised Land, but He is motivating them to restore its ancient wealth as it was in the days of David and Solomon.

In the next chapter we will examine a number of specific prophecies as well as the words of Jesus Himself that provide prophetic signposts of how quickly we are approaching the final crisis — the return of Jesus Christ to set up His kingdom.

■ ■ ■ ■

Five:
The Third Temple in
the Last Days

HOW PLANS TO BUILD THE TEMPLE SIGNAL
CHRIST'S SOON RETURN

■ ■ ■ ■

In that day will I raise up the tabernacle of
    David
that is fallen,
and close up the breaches thereof;
and I will raise up his ruins,
and I will build it as in the days of old.

Amos 9:11

The holy Temple in Jerusalem was the focus of Jewish spiritual life in Israel in the centuries before its destruction by the Roman legions in AD 70. For almost two thousand years the Temple has been lost to the Jews, yet it has remained central to their aspirations. Over the centuries the Jews have prayed that God would allow them to restore their sacred sanctuary in the last days leading to the appearance of the long-awaited Messiah.

Throughout the Old and New Testaments, the prophets of God repeatedly declared that the Temple would be rebuilt and would play a significant role in the events of the last days. Three of the most important Old Testament prophets — Micah, Amos, and Haggai — prepared the Jewish people to anticipate the rebuilding of the Temple.

The prophet Amos, whose name in Hebrew means "God will judge injustice," was a shepherd living near Bethlehem who prophesied to the ten northern tribes of Israel in 760 BC. Following the reign of Solomon, Israel had been divided into two kingdoms. The southern kingdom, Judah, was composed of the tribes of Judah and Benjamin. The northern kingdom, Israel, was made up of the ten other tribes. Although Amos lived in Judah, the Lord inspired him to address his prophecy to the northern kingdom. Amos prophesied that the Lord would cause the Temple to be rebuilt in Jerusalem in the last days: "In that day will I raise up the tabernacle of David that is fallen, and close up the breaches thereof; and I will raise up his ruins, and I will build it as in the days of old" (Amos 9:11).

The prophet Micah (740 BC), who lived southwest of Jerusalem during the reigns of King Ahaz and King Hezekiah, wrote about the future Third Temple: "But in the last days it shall come to pass, that the mountain of the house of the LORD shall be established in the top of the mountains, and it shall be exalted above the hills; and people shall flow unto it" (Micah 4:1). Two centuries later Haggai (520 BC), who lived during the reign of the Persian king Darius, ministered to the Jewish exiles who chose to return to Israel after seventy years of captivity in Babylon. Haggai foretold, "The glory of this latter house shall be greater than of the former, saith the LORD of hosts" (Haggai 2:9). His prophecy appears to refer to the Second Temple. However, it also seems to look further into the future to the building of the Third Temple, which will be defiled by the Antichrist and then cleansed and purified by the return of the Messiah.

Daniel prophesied that the rebuilt Temple would serve as the center of Israel's worship — complete with the resumption of the ancient animal-sacrifice system. In his famous vision of the seventy weeks (see Daniel 9:24–27), he predicted that the last great world dictator — the Antichrist — would arise within the area of the ancient Roman Empire and would eventually rule the revived empire, including Western Europe, North Africa, and the Middle East (Daniel 2:40–45; 7:7–8). He declared that this world dictator would sign a seven-year security treaty (covenant) with Israel: "And he shall confirm the covenant with many for one week: and in the midst of the week he shall cause the sacrifice and the oblation to cease" (Daniel 9:27). After only three and a half years, the world leader would arbitrarily violate the treaty, and at that time the Antichrist would enter the Holy of Holies, defiling the rebuilt Temple.

Obviously, the Antichrist cannot stop (or cause "to cease") the daily sacrifices unless, prior to that moment, the Corban — the daily morning and evening sacrificial system — has been reinstated. The last daily sacrifice of sheep occurred three weeks before the burning of the Temple in the summer of AD 70. At that time the Roman legions surrounded the Second Temple and prevented lambs from being brought in for the sacrifice. Before Daniel's prophecy can be fulfilled, the Jews must reinstate daily animal sacrifice. An altar will be built in the area to the east of the site for the Third Temple. Once the priests resume the daily sacrifices, the construction of the Temple itself will begin.

As Jesus met with His disciples, He unfolded a number of significant prophecies that would, by their fulfillment, set the stage for the events of a critical seven-year period. This period, known as the Tribulation Week, will begin with the Antichrist signing a security treaty with Israel (see Daniel 9:27).

Jesus warned His disciples about the coming Antichrist, the world leader who would establish a global dictatorship under Satan's leadership. Jesus quoted the prophet Daniel: "When ye therefore shall see the abomination of desolation, spoken of by Daniel the prophet, stand in the holy place, (whoso readeth, let him understand:) Then let them which be in Judaea flee into the mountains" (Matthew 24:15–16). The "abomination of desolation" refers to Satan, in the body of the Antichrist, defiling the Holy of Holies when he enters the Temple. After this abomination is carried out, the False Prophet, who is the partner of the Antichrist, will demand that the world's population worship the Antichrist as "god" in the Temple. Daniel's and Christ's prophecies suggest that the Third Temple will first be built so these prophecies can be fulfilled.

The apostle Paul also prophesied that the Antichrist will defile the Third Temple. Paul declared that the Lord Jesus Christ will not return to establish His kingdom on earth until "that man of sin," the Antichrist, is first revealed as "the son of perdition; who opposeth and exalteth himself above all that is called God, or that is worshipped; so that he as God sitteth in the temple of God, shewing himself that he is God" (2 Thessalonians 2:3–4). While some have taught that the Third Temple will be built by the Antichrist, both Paul (2 Thessalonians 2:3–4) and John (Revelation 11:1–2) describe the

Third Temple as "the temple of God," suggesting that it will be rebuilt by the Jews as a genuine Holy Temple.

The small nation of Israel and especially the holy city of Jerusalem are at the center of the world's most volatile spiritual, political, and military conflict. The fulfillment of dozens of Messianic prophecies in our lifetime strongly suggests that our generation will witness the rebuilding of the Temple, the battle of Armageddon, and the return of Christ. The final Armageddon struggle for the destiny of humanity will be waged in the Valley of Jezreel, which lies to the east of the mount of Megiddo in northern Israel.

Virtually all prophecy teachers agree that the preconditions for the rebuilding of the Temple and the return of Jesus Christ, together with the current religious developments in Israel, are setting the stage for the new Temple. For the last three decades the Temple Institute, a small but very dedicated group of orthodox rabbis, has been working quietly in the Old City of Jerusalem to train Levite priests and to re-create the ancient Temple worship vessels and musical instruments. These are essential for authentic worship in the new sanctuary. In addition, many in the Orthodox Jewish religious leadership throughout Israel now support the efforts under way to prepare for construction of the Third Temple.

BUILDING THE THIRD TEMPLE

God declared throughout the Scriptures that the Temple must be rebuilt before the Messiah returns to earth and cleanses the sanctuary. Both of these events will occur in the generation that witnessed the return of the Jews to their Promised Land in 1948. King David prophesied, "When the LORD shall build up Zion, he shall appear in his glory" (Psalm 102:16). Jesus promised His disciples that the generation that witnessed the budding of the fig tree (the rebirth of Israel) would also see the coming of the Son of Man. Christ declared, "Now learn a parable of the fig tree; When his branch is yet tender, and putteth forth leaves, ye know that summer is nigh: So likewise ye, when ye shall see all these things, know that it is near, even at the doors. Verily I say unto you, This generation shall not pass, till all these things be fulfilled" (Matthew 24:32–34). The fig tree was well known as a symbol of Israel, as the eagle is a symbol of America and the maple leaf a symbol of Canada.

In ancient Israel a political generation was

considered to be a period of forty years. For example, the following judges and kings of Israel ruled for forty years: Moses; the judges Othniel, Deborah, and Gideon; and the kings David, Solomon, Jeroboam II, and Joash. However, according to Psalm 90:10 the length of a typical lifetime or a natural generation is seventy to eighty years: "The days of our years are threescore years and ten; and if by reason of strength they be fourscore years . . ." The most natural and logical interpretation of Christ's prophecy about the generation is that those who were alive in 1948 (including many readers of this book) will see the fulfillment of prophecies regarding the rebuilding of the Temple and Christ's return. Most people who were very young during Israel's 1948 War of Independence are still alive today, so in light of prophecy, most of this generation could see the Third Temple built (see Micah 4:1–2).

Throughout the last two millenniums, many Jewish and Christian scholars have doubted that the Temple will ever be rebuilt. One major obstacle was the fact that the Sanhedrin, the highest court of Jewish religious lawmakers, had ceased to exist almost fifteen centuries ago. The Sanhedrin must exist in order to reestablish the authentic Levitical priesthood, to train priests in the ancient rituals of Temple animal sacrifice, to determine the appropriate religious rituals, and to identify the precise, correct location for rebuilding the Temple.

Besides the reconstitution of the Sanhedrin and the training of the priesthood, both of which are now under way, numerous other obstacles remain, including the loss of the sacred utensils of Temple worship. But the greatest obstacle is the tremendous political, religious, and possibly military strife that would almost inevitably arise in the Arab and Muslim world in response to any Jewish building project on the Temple Mount. A move to break ground for the Third Temple would certainly risk inciting a brutal global jihad (a holy war). A small foretaste of this conflict occurred during the violent Muslim rioting on the Temple Mount in the spring of 2007 in response to Israel's excavations to rebuild the main access ramp to the mount, even though the excavation was 165 feet from the nearest Islamic sacred site.

But despite the Islamic and Arab opposition to any Jewish building on the Temple Mount, the Lord prophesied that the Jewish exiles would, in the last days, return to their Promised Land and rebuild the Temple. As the prophet Ezekiel declared:

> I will make a covenant of peace with them;
> it shall be an everlasting covenant with
> them: and I will place them, and multiply
> them, and will set my sanctuary in the
> midst of them for evermore. My tabernacle
> also shall be with them: yea, I will be their
> God, and they shall be my people. And
> the heathen shall know that I the LORD do
> sanctify Israel, when my sanctuary shall
> be in the midst of them for evermore.
> (Ezekiel 37:26–28)

Moses Maimonides, also known as Rambam (c. 1200), was one of the greatest Jewish rabbis. Maimonides taught that the Holy Temple revealed the divine nature of God and His eternal covenant relationship to Israel. He declared that the 613 separate mitzvot (commandments) found throughout the five books of Moses, the Torah, include God's direct command to Israel to build the Temple (see Exodus 25:8–9). Maimonides noted that this divine commandment was never rescinded. Therefore he taught that the rabbis living in exile in every generation should study and teach the sacred texts that deal with the Temple and its worship. These teachings would look ahead to the day when the Jews would once again possess Israel and the city of Jerusalem. Only then could they fulfill God's command to "make me a sanctuary." In our generation the exiles have returned to the Promised Land and have been given both the opportunity and the prophetic task of fulfilling the nation's ancient dream.

Israel's stunning victory over its Arab enemies during the Six-Day War in early June 1967 reestablished Jewish sovereignty over the united city of Jerusalem for the first time in almost two thousand years. In response to Israel's remarkable victory in only one hundred hours of fierce battles, *Time* magazine published an article with the headline "Should the Temple Be Rebuilt?" The writer asked this provocative question: "Assuming that Israel keeps the [Western] Wall, which is one of the few remaining ruins of Judaism's Second Temple, has the time now come for the erection of the Third Temple? . . . Some Jews see plausible theological grounds for discussing reconstruction. They base their argument on the contention that Israel has already entered its 'Messianic Era.' "[1]

Rabbi Maimonides wrote his multivolume *Mishneh Torah,* the greatest codification of Jewish and biblical law, which concluded with a fourteenth volume titled *Hilchos Bais HaBechirah* (The Laws of God's Chosen House). The book contains six key mitzvot that summarize the Lord's laws given to Israel regarding the Temple:

> The Jews are to build a sanctuary.
> They are to build the altar with stone that is not hewn.
> They are not to ascend the altar with steps; they must use a ramp.
> They must fear and reverence the Temple.
> They must guard the Temple completely.
> They must never cease watching over the Temple.[2]

During the 1990s Rabbi Eliyahu Touger wrote a new translation of the *Mishneh Torah.* In his introduction to the fourteenth volume, Touger wrote, "As the text was being composed, we would frequently tell each other: 'Work faster. At any moment, Moshiach may come and rebuild the Temple. Who knows how this book will sell then?' "[3]

Although the conquest of the Old City of Jerusalem made it possible for the Jews to rebuild the Temple, until recently only a small percentage of the Jews in Israel expressed support for the idea. After Israel's independence was declared on May 15,

1948, the chief rabbi declared that, with the reestablishment of the Jewish state and the ingathering of the exiles, "the age of redemption" had begun. The historian Israel Eldad wrote that the sanctuary would be rebuilt in our generation: "We are at the stage where David was when he liberated Jerusalem; from that time until the construction of the Temple of Solomon, only one generation passed, so will it be with us."[4]

The question remains: what would possibly motivate the current non-religious political leadership of Israel to overcome the obstacles to rebuilding the Temple? I believe that prophecy suggests God will change the hearts and minds of Israel's leadership as well as the Islamic-Arab world in the aftermath of the supernatural defeat of the Russian-Islamic armies during the War of Gog and Magog, described in Ezekiel 38–39. A military alliance composed of huge armies from Russia, Eastern Europe, former states in the U.S.S.R., Iran, North Africa, Ethiopia, and the Arab-Islamic nations will gather to annihilate the Jews. However, the prophecy of Ezekiel reveals that God will supernaturally destroy this enormous military force. A second development that could radically change the hearts of Israel's leaders would be the recovery of the long-lost ark of the covenant. This would provide a powerful motive to rebuild the Temple, since the original purpose of both the Tabernacle and the Temple was to provide a sanctuary for the ark. In chapter 8 we will look in detail at the probable location and future role of the ark of the covenant and the events that might allow it to be returned to the rebuilt Temple.

New Findings Related to the Temple's Original Location

The ancient Dome of the Rock is located almost dead center on the thirty-five acre Temple Mount. This beautiful octagonal building was completed by Caliph Abdal-Malik in AD 691, following the Arab conquest of Palestine. Assuming this Islamic prayer shrine was built on the foundation of the First and Second Temples, a number of prophecy students concluded that the ancient Muslim shrine would have to be removed or destroyed before the Temple could be rebuilt. If so, it would be virtually impossible for Israel to ever build the Third Temple.

However, my studies suggest that the rebuilt Temple and the existing Islamic structures, including the Dome of the Rock

Temple Mount

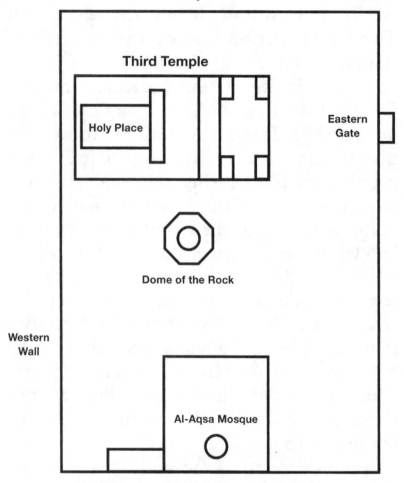

Third Temple

Holy Place

Eastern Gate

Dome of the Rock

Western Wall

Al-Aqsa Mosque

This diagram shows the future location of the Third Temple in what is now an open area directly to the north of the Dome of the Rock.

and the Al-Aqsa Mosque, will coexist on the Temple Mount during the seven-year Tribulation Period leading to the battle of Armageddon. A careful reading of John's prophecy in Revelation indicates that the Dome of the Rock and the Temple will both occupy the Temple Mount, without any disruption of the Muslim shrine. John prophesied that during a period after the rebuilding of the Temple, a large part of the Temple Mount to the south of the Temple, known as the Court of the Gentiles (which is outside the inner Temple proper), will remain under the control of the Gentiles (Muslims). This will continue for forty-two months (three and a half years), until Christ returns to set up His millennial kingdom. This will follow His victory over the Antichrist and False Prophet at the end of the battle of Armageddon.

In John's vision of the seven-year Tribulation period, including the final three and a half years leading up to the battle of Armageddon, the prophet was told by the angel: "Rise, and measure the temple of God, and the altar, and them that worship therein. But the court which is without the temple leave out, and measure it not; for it is given unto the Gentiles: and the holy city shall they tread under foot forty and two months"

(Revelation 11:1–2).

During the last few years Jewish archaeologists have made fascinating discoveries on and beneath the Temple Mount that pinpoint the original site of Solomon's Temple and therefore the location for the Third Temple (see diagram). The site is an open area directly north of the Dome of the Rock. After Israel's recapture of the Mount in June 1967, Israeli archaeologists began to dig a nine-hundred-yard-long tunnel proceeding north along the Western Wall, underneath the thousand-year-old Muslim structures. This tunnel is almost sixty-five feet below the present-day streets and basements in the Muslim Quarter of the Old City.

The tunnel exposed a number of ancient gates to the Temple that had been hidden for almost two thousand years by rubble the Roman soldiers had thrown into the valley beside the Western Wall. The position of these ancient gates supports the theory that the original Temple and the Second Temple, where Christ taught, were in fact directly opposite the Eastern Gate.

When Jewish archaeologists excavated the area, they exposed massive foundation stones from the Second Temple and some deep foundation blocks that may have existed since the First Temple. Several of the carved limestone blocks measure forty-six feet by twenty feet by ten feet. They weigh from four hundred to one thousand tons each and fit so closely together that you cannot place a razor blade between them (In comparison, the largest stones used in the Great Pyramid seldom exceed fifty tons.) We know of no modern technology using cranes or helicopters that could transport such massive blocks of stone over one mile from the quarry to the Temple Mount.

The most significant confirmation of the true location of the Temple comes from two critical sources. First, Ezekiel foretold that the Messiah would supernaturally enter the rebuilt Temple through the now-sealed Eastern Gate: "And the glory of the LORD [the Messiah] came into the house [Temple] by the way of the gate whose prospect is toward the east [the previously sealed Eastern Gate]" (Ezekiel 43:4). Since all known ancient temple structures in the Middle East place the temple structure directly behind the major entrance gate leading worshipers within the sacred structure, we can conclude that the rebuilt Temple will be located in a direct east-west line from the massive gate complex known as the Eastern Gate. The *Jewish Mishneh* records that the Eastern Gate led directly into the Beautiful Gate of the inner Second Temple.

A further confirmation of the Temple being located north of the Dome of the Rock comes from the *Mishneh Torah,* which reveals that on the day of the sacrifice of the red heifer, a young priest stood on the plateau of the Mount of Olives. He led a red heifer across a stone bridge composed of arches upon arches that went from the Temple's Eastern Gate eastward across the Kidron Valley to the midlevel plateau on the Mount of Olives. It was there that the sacrifice of the red heifer and the burning of the ashes took place. The priest looked across the valley through a low gap in the Temple Mount wall directly above the Eastern Gate and through the open Beautiful Gate and saw the sacred veil of the inner temple. This could occur only if the original Temple was located in a direct east-west line to the west of the Eastern Gate.

James Fleming, a respected teacher working at a college near Bethlehem, was photographing the sealed Eastern Gate in April 1969. A prolonged rainy period had softened the ground in front of the gate, an area occupied by a century-old Arab cemetery.

As Fleming walked backward taking a photo of the sealed gate, the ground gave way, causing him to fall unconscious into an ancient necropolis. He awoke a few minutes later lying a dozen feet underground, surrounded by gravestones and skeletons. To his amazement, directly in front of him was the arch of the original Eastern Gate that was part of the First Temple wall. The subterranean Eastern Gate is beneath the present sealed Eastern Gate. This confirms that the ancient gate was located in the very same spot as the current gate.[5] Almost two thousand years after the destruction of the Second Temple, we can now be confident where the Temple once stood — directly to the west of the sealed Eastern Gate. The Third Temple can be built on the exact location of Solomon's Temple.

ISRAEL'S REBIRTH AND THE THIRD TEMPLE

Isaiah foretold that the Temple of God would stand again in the latter days: "And it shall come to pass in the last days, that the mountain of the LORD's house shall be established in the top of the mountains, and shall be exalted above the hills; and all nations shall flow unto it" (Isaiah 2:2). In 1948 the dream of almost fifty generations of Jewish exiles was fulfilled when the chief rabbi ordered the shofar (ram's horn) blown in recognition that the hour of redemption was at hand. The chief rabbis stated that the reestablishment of the Jewish state and the ingathering of the exiles meant "the age of redemption" had begun.[6]

The prophetic clock started ticking in the countdown to the Messiah's return. Israel, the "fig tree" of Christ's prophecy, was reborn in 1948. And according to Jesus' prophecy, the generation living when Israel was reborn can hope to live to see the return of Christ (see Matthew 24:32–34).

Some readers will naturally ask how we can be certain that the fig tree putting forth leaves is God's prophetic symbol of Israel's rebirth. In both the Old and New Testaments, the symbol of the fig tree is used exclusively for Israel (see Judges 9:10; 1 Kings 4:25; Luke 13:7; John 1:50). A very early Jewish-Christian commentary on Jesus' Mount of Olives prophecy, the *Apocalypse of Peter* (AD 110), addresses the identity of the fig tree. When the writer of the commentary asks the rhetorical question, What is the fig tree? the answer is given: "It is the nation and house of Israel."[7] Within forty years of the destruction of the Temple, early Jewish Christians understood that Christ predicted Israel (though at that time desolate) would be reborn as a nation in the generation when the Messiah would return.

CAN GENTILES HELP REBUILD THE TEMPLE?

In November 1990 a group of Israeli government representatives, architects, engineers, rabbis, lawyers, and archaeologists met to discuss solutions to the practical problems in rebuilding the Temple. They estimated it would take one to two years to build the basic Temple structure. Naturally, the final decorations and finishing details would take ten to twenty years, as it did with the Second Temple. In the days of Christ, the craftsmen had been working on the decorative gold work and wood carving of Herod's reconstruction of the Temple for forty-six years. "Then said the Jews, Forty and six years was this temple in building, and wilt thou rear it up in three days?" (John 2:20).

For the first time since AD 70, the leaders of the Orthodox Jews in Israel are seriously considering the practical steps required to rebuild the Temple. Each year a growing percentage of the population believes that Israel must build the Third Temple to demonstrate to the world (and especially the Arab-Islamic world) that the Jews will stay in Jerusalem and Israel forever.

Today many evangelical and charismatic Christians are among the strongest supporters of Israel, and many of us believe in Israel's right to rebuild the Temple. During my discussions with Jewish religious groups and individuals in Israel, the question of whether Gentiles can help rebuild the Temple often comes up. Based on the biblical account of the Gentiles providing manpower, craftsmen, and materials for Solomon's Temple, it seems there is no fundamental problem in Gentiles helping build the Third Temple. When I asked several Levites and Orthodox Jews in Jerusalem why they were so cooperative in discussing research questions about the Temple project, they sometimes replied they had an ancient tradition that Gentiles would assist in the last days to rebuild the sanctuary.

The prophet Zechariah declared that in the millennial kingdom "every one that is left of all the nations [Gentiles] which came against Jerusalem shall even go up from year to year to worship the King, the LORD of hosts, and to keep the feast of tabernacles" (Zechariah 14:16).

For thousands of years devout Jews have

prayed toward Jerusalem three times every day, asking the Lord to return the Divine Shekinah Presence to the rebuilt Temple. After many centuries we have come to the final generation that has been given the task of transforming these ancient dreams into reality.

■ ■ ■ ■

Six:
Practical
Preparations for
Rebuilding the
Temple

RECONVENING THE SANHEDRIN,
RECOVERING THE OIL OF ANOINTING,
AND PREPARING FOR THE
RED-HEIFER SACRIFICE

■ ■ ■ ■

And many people shall go and say,
Come ye, and let us go up to the mountain
of the LORD,
to the house of the God of Jacob;
and he will teach us of his ways,

and we will walk in his paths:
for out of Zion shall go forth the law,
and the word of the LORD from Jerusalem.

Isaiah 2:3

The Sanhedrin was the highest court in ancient Israel. They were given the right to rule on all religious issues and disputes for the nation and the right to determine the rules for Temple worship.

Before Israel can rebuild the Temple, the ancient Sanhedrin must be reestablished. The original Sanhedrin court met for the last time in AD 453 in the town of Tiberias, Israel, on the western side of the Sea of Galilee. But in these last days, the Sanhedrin must be reconvened to issue necessary rulings regarding sacred rituals, sacrifices, qualifications for membership in the Temple Levitical priesthood, and other matters pertaining to the rebuilding of the Temple and the restoration of authentic Temple worship.

In accordance with the rules specified by Rabbi Moses Maimonides (AD 1200), seventy-one of the most highly respected rabbis in Israel received special ordination as the new Sanhedrin on October 13, 2004. The new Sanhedrin includes Orthodox Jewish leaders from every part of Israel, including two former chief rabbis of Israel — Ovadiah Josef, the former chief rabbi of the Sephardic Jews (Middle Eastern Jews), and Josef Elyashiv, the former chief rabbi of the Ashkenazi Jews (European Jews). Rabbi Elyashiv is considered by many of the top rabbis in Israel to be the true spiritual heir of Moses and therefore was in a position of spiritual authority to ordain the seventy other religious leaders required for a full Sanhedrin court.

The re-creation of the Sanhedrin was an unprecedented step in the practical preparations for building a new Temple. Other vital preconditions include the re-creation of almost one hundred sacred Temple vessels used in worship and in the ceremonial cleansing of the Temple. Another requirement is the recovery of the sacred oil used in the anointing of priests and, ultimately, the coming Messiah. Of special interest in this regard is the discovery of ancient ceremonial oil of anointing and the search for the ashes from the last sacrifice of a red heifer. Also of interest is the recovery of necessary ingredients for making a unique deep blue dye required for the special priestly garments, especially the high priest's robes.

THE NEW SANHEDRIN

The Sanhedrin (a name derived from a Greek word meaning "assembly") began thirty-five hundred years ago during the Exodus from Egypt. In recognition that Moses was exhausting himself trying to judge the affairs of the people on his own, God commanded Moses to assemble seventy elders from all the tribes to share the responsibility. This assembly would lead the nation (see Numbers 11:16–17). The Sanhedrin council or court — seventy-one leaders appointed from the twelve tribes — held all legislative and judicial powers from the time of the Exodus (approximately 1490 BC) until the Babylonian army destroyed Israel's sovereignty and burned the First Temple in 586 BC. When the Jewish exiles returned to Jerusalem from Babylon seventy years later, Ezra reinstituted the Great Sanhedrin to provide spiritual leadership and guidance before the people began to rebuild the Temple (516 BC).

The modern-day Sanhedrin was formally convened in Jerusalem on January 20, 2005. The court's leader, Rabbi Yeshai Ba'avad, declared that the rabbinic body would meet monthly to issue religious legal rulings, saying, "This is the need of the generation and of the hour."[1] Rabbi Yisrael Ariel, the head of the Temple Institute and a key Sanhedrin member, stated, "Our Talmudic Sages describe the ten stages of exile of the Sanhedrin from Jerusalem to other locations, until it ended in Tiberias — and this [Tiberias, where the current members were ordained in 2004] is the place where it was foretold that it would be renewed, and from here it will be relocated to Jerusalem."[2]

The reconstituted Sanhedrin discussed several key ideas related to building the Third Temple, including the construction of an altar that would be used for the sacrifice of a lamb during a future Passover. Hundreds of priests from the tribe of Levi were authorized to begin training in the precise rituals of the ancient Temple sacrifices. They also discussed Rabbi Ben-Yosef's concept of reinstating the Sanhedrin's religious authority by announcing Rosh Hodesh, the day that marks the beginning of each lunar month. "It is very important to reinstate the Sanhedrin's authority to announce the month, because it will force people to understand that God gave us the power to control the calendar and our own destiny," according to Ben-Yosef, a leading member of the new Sanhedrin.[3]

Additional Sanhedrin meetings were convened in January 2005 to discuss the appropriate rules for rebuilding the Temple and the resumption of Temple worship. In June 2005 Rabbi Adin Steinsaltz was elected temporary president of the resurrected Sanhedrin. The assembly is now dealing with a number of critical issues, including the original location of the First and Second Temples and hence where the new Temple must be built, rebuilding the altar of sacrifice, restoration of the Davidic monarchy, the determination of the precise length of the biblical cubit, and the return of the ten lost tribes to Israel.

In February 2005 the Sanhedrin considered the three logical possibilities for the historical location of the First and Second Temples.[4] The first possibility: Solomon's Temple was centered with its Holy of Holies on the rock that today sits within the thirteen-hundred-year-old Dome of the Rock. The second possibility: Solomon's Temple was located to the north of the Dome of the Rock on an east-west line directly opposite the Eastern Gate. The third possibility: the Temple was built to the south of the Dome of the Rock near the location of the Al-Aqsa Mosque, close to the southern wall of the Temple Mount.

A Sanhedrin subcommittee is considering the archaeological, historical, and theological evidence, as well as the implications, of the eventual determination of the Temple's correct location. The second possible location (north of the Dome of the Rock), which I believe is supported by Scripture, the *Mishneh Torah,* and significant archaeological discoveries, would make it possible for the Israelis to build the Third Temple in an open area directly to the west of the sealed Eastern Gate (see photograph).

The sealed Eastern Gate can be seen in the center of this photograph of the Temple Mount. An open area to the west of this gate is the most likely site for building the Third Temple.

The rabbinical council that initiated the reestablishment of the Sanhedrin called on all Jewish groups involved in research on the rebuilding of the Temple to submit detailed architectural plans in preparation for the construction project.[5] WorldNetDaily.com reported that the Sanhedrin itself "will establish a forum of architects and engineers to begin plans for rebuilding the Temple — a move fraught with religious and political volatility."[6]

In addition, practical preparations by the Sanhedrin include issuing a call for donors to contribute funds to acquire building materials. (Costing billions, the Third Temple will certainly be the most expensive construction project in history.) One of the more intriguing requests is the requirement for assistance in "the gathering and preparation of prefabricated, disassembled portions to be stored and ready for rapid assembly, 'in the manner of King David.' "[7] It is significant that God told David to quarry the stones off site and then transport the quarried limestone blocks to the Temple Mount. There they would be assembled silently, in respect of the sanctity of the structure. Similarly, the new Sanhedrin plans to quarry the necessary material off site and then quickly assemble the stones in silence on the Temple Mount when God provides a sign that the time has come.

The senior spokesman for the Sanhedrin, Rabbi Chaim Richman, an extremely knowledgeable scholar regarding the Temple, a man I have met and interviewed on several occasions, declared to the Israeli media source Arutz-7: "The Sanhedrin is researching ways to renew the deepest roots of our faith — to renew Temple service, reunite Jewish legal tradition and inspire the Jewish people to aspire to greatness. Our people have one path before us, and we will continue to march toward our destiny."[8]

A number of Jewish rabbis and scholars have argued that it is presumptuous for Jews to make plans to rebuild the Temple before the Messiah appears. Many Jewish scholars believe that the Scriptures and Talmud both declare that the Messiah will be the one to rebuild the Temple. They point to the words of the prophet Zechariah: "And speak unto him, saying, Thus speaketh the LORD of hosts, saying, Behold the man whose name is The BRANCH; and he shall grow up out of his place, and he shall build the temple of the LORD: Even he shall build the temple of the LORD" (Zechariah 6:12–13). Zechariah's prophecy of the Messiah's role in building the Temple refers to the enormous millennial Temple that will be constructed following the battle of Armageddon. Therefore, there is no contradiction between Zechariah's prophecy of the Messiah building the Fourth Temple during the Millennium and the numerous other prophecies in both the Old and New Testaments that refer to the Jews of Israel building the Third Temple prior to the Antichrist defiling the sanctuary during the Tribulation.

Maimonides wrote in his *Letter on Religious Persecution:* "Not one of any of the commandments of the Torah is dependent upon the Messiah's arrival."[9] Therefore, in light of the fact that many of the 613 commandments itemized in the Talmud deal with Temple worship, it logically follows from Maimonides' teaching that the Third Temple could and, in fact, will be rebuilt before the appearance of the Messiah. This confirming statement is found in the *Jerusalem Talmud:* "The [third] Holy Temple will in the future be re-established before the establishment of the kingdom of David."[10]

THE OIL OF ANOINTING

God provided detailed instructions not just regarding the construction of the Tabernacle (and later the Temple) but also regarding the worship vessels to be used. The oil of anointing was to be used to anoint the Tabernacle, Aaron as high priest, and the sacred objects of worship: "And thou shalt anoint the tabernacle of the congregation therewith, and the ark of the testimony. . . . And thou shalt anoint Aaron and his sons, and consecrate them, that they may minister unto me in the priest's office. And thou shalt speak unto the children of Israel, saying, This shall be an holy anointing oil unto me throughout your generations" (Exodus 30:26, 30–31).

After being used in the Tabernacle and later in the First and Second Temples, the oil of anointing disappeared when the Romans destroyed the Second Temple. According to the Talmud, the oil is composed of "five hundred shekels of flowing myrrh, five hundred of cassia, five hundred of sweet cinnamon and two hundred and fifty of sweet calamus, together one thousand seven hundred and fifty shekels."[11] This formula is very similar to the list of ingredients given to Moses (see Exodus 30:23–25).

This same oil of anointing is crucial in the last days because it will be needed to anoint the Messiah when He appears. Daniel predicted that the ushering in of the kingdom of God would include the anointing of "the most Holy," the long-awaited Messiah of Israel. Daniel wrote, "Seventy weeks are determined upon thy people and upon thy holy city, to finish the transgression, and to make an end of sins, and to make reconciliation for iniquity, and to bring in everlasting righteousness, and to seal up the vision and prophecy, and *to anoint the most Holy*" (Daniel 9:24).

I believe that we may witness the oil of anointing being used by the high priest of Israel to anoint Jesus the Messiah when He returns to the Temple to establish His kingdom. It is important to note that Jesus of Nazareth was never anointed during His life on earth. His Hebrew title is Moshiach, which means "Messiah" or "Anointed One." The name Christ (*christos* in Greek) means "the anointed of God" and conveys the same prophetic truth that Jesus will one day be anointed by oil as the true King of Israel.

As we discussed in an earlier chapter, the two chief rabbis of Israel are in possession of the ancient clay jar that contains the oil of anointing from the time of the Second Temple. This makes it possible for Daniel's prophecy of the anointing of the coming Messiah to be fulfilled. It is one of the most significant prophetic developments in our generation, pointing to the imminent coming of the Messiah.

RECOVERING THE BLUE DYE FOR THE GARMENTS OF THE HIGH PRIEST

The Bible and the *Mishneh Torah* both emphasize the necessity of using a certain rare, blue dye to create the beautiful robes of the high priest (see Exodus 28:31). The Bible records that many of the special garments, including the *avnet*-belt of the high priest, must be dyed with a special blue dye known as *tchelet*. But since the days of the Second Temple, crucial ingredients of the dye have been lost. Several manuscripts were written by Jewish scholars, including the late chief rabbi Isaac Herzog, about the lost dye and the seeming impossibility of resuming authentic Temple worship due to the absence of the required dye.[12]

This dye was produced from a rare mollusk found only in the Mediterranean Sea, a marine creature long thought to be extinct. However, in the late 1990s Israeli divers discovered the mollusk, the hillazon snail (*Murex trunculus*), in the Red Sea.

A thick liquid is extracted from a gland in the mollusk to produce the rich blue dye. The Temple Institute in Jerusalem has created a supply of the blue dye, which will be used to create the garments required in

Temple worship. The unspun wool for the priestly robe is dipped in this liquid, turning the wool a bright green. When the now-green wool is exposed to light, it takes on a rich blue color. Once it dries, the wool is spun by craftsmen into a blue thread that is incorporated into the garments worn by the high priest.

Several years ago a representative of the Temple Institute gave me some linen that was dipped in the rare blue dye. In the Temple Institute they have on display the snail that produces the dye. This blue dye also is used to produce the *tsitsit* fringes worn by observant Jewish males in the Temple.

THE ASHES OF THE RED HEIFER

The Third Temple cannot be built and used for worship until the appropriate area on the Temple Mount is ritually purified using waters of purification from the ashes of an unblemished red heifer. "Speak unto the children of Israel, that they bring thee a red heifer without spot, wherein is no blemish, and upon which never came yoke" (Numbers 19:2). According to the Torah, the Talmud, and the rabbis, it is essential for Israel to resume the sacrifice of the ashes of the red heifer in order to produce the waters of purification needed to ritually cleanse the Temple Mount, the sacred vessels, and the Levitical priesthood in preparation for rebuilding the Temple. Ezekiel prophesied the rebirth of Israel and the resumption of the waters of purification from the red heifer in the last days (see Ezekiel 36:25).

The two chief rabbis of Israel told *Time* magazine in 1989 that the Third Temple could not be built until they could complete the sacrifice of the ashes of the red heifer.[13] This is essential because everything, including the Temple's foundation stones, was defiled by sin and the presumed defiling presence of dead men's bones in the earth below. Only the waters of purification from the red-heifer ashes could purify the Temple site.

Israel's religious leaders authorized a team to locate and raise a breed of pure-red cattle. Appropriate cattle were found in Finland and the United States. Once they choose a red heifer without any blemishes, they will sacrifice it on the Mount of Olives opposite the Eastern Gate. The ashes from the burned sacrifice will be mixed with water, scarlet thread, cedar, and hyssop, producing the waters of purification. Then the priest will sprinkle the water on the stones of the Temple Mount, the priests, and the Temple vessels according to the Bible's commands as recorded in Numbers 19.

A pure-red heifer is very rare. Almost all cattle have some imperfections in their coloring. The Talmud states that even one white or black hair would disqualify the heifer. Not only does the heifer have to be completely red, it could never have had a yoke laid upon its neck. In addition, it must have no blemishes or wounds. The Mishneh (Parah 1:2) declares that the red heifer should be a female between two and four years of age, of pure-red hair with no double white or black hairs springing from one follicle, and having never been put to work, not even having a cloth placed on its back.

Jewish authorities are raising a number of red heifers in Israel so they will have a qualified candidate when they receive a divine sign that the time has finally come to rebuild the Temple. In fact, Israeli newspapers reported in May 1997 that a pure-red heifer was born in Israel that met the qualifications described in Numbers 19.[14]

The red-heifer sacrifice itself is paradoxical. While the aim of the sacrifice originally was to ritually purify priests and sacred objects from spiritual defilement resulting from contact with death, the act of participating in the sacrifice of the red heifer spiritually defiled all who were involved. One commentary states, "It [the sacrifice] purifies the impure, and at the same time renders impure the pure!"[15] So inscrutable was the nature of this sacrifice that the rabbis wrote in the Talmud that even King Solomon despaired of learning the spiritual mystery of the red-heifer commandments. Solomon apparently could not understand why Numbers 19 declared that the priest who obediently offered the red heifer would himself become sinfully defiled or unclean until evening.

Moses recorded God's command to Israel regarding the red-heifer sacrifice, which specifies:

This is the ordinance of the law which the LORD hath commanded, saying, Speak unto the children of Israel, that they bring thee a red heifer without spot, wherein is no blemish, and upon which never came yoke. . . . And one shall burn the heifer in his [the priest's] sight; her skin, and her flesh, and her blood, with her dung, shall he burn. . . . And a man that is clean shall gather up the ashes of the heifer, and lay them up without the camp in a clean place, and it shall be kept for the congregation of the children of Israel for a water of separation: it is a purification for sin. (Numbers 19:2, 5, 9)

The defilement from contact with the dead was called tumas ohel. The spiritual defilement continued for seven days and prevented anyone contaminated from participating in the community, marriages, and especially Temple worship unless he was ritually cleansed according to the instructions in Numbers 19, which require a Levite priest applying with hyssop the waters of purification on the contaminated person. All the Levitical rules of defilement are related to some degree to the person's connection to the death of a body.

During the Exodus, after the red heifer was sacrificed outside the camp, its blood was sprinkled toward the Holy Place by a priest standing opposite the entrance to the Tabernacle. When Solomon built the Temple five centuries later, the sacrifice of the red heifer occurred on a plateau on the western slope of the Mount of Olives in direct view of the Holy of Holies. This small plateau was directly across the Kidron Valley opposite the Eastern Gate. During a research trip to Israel, I followed the precise eyewitness description found in the *Mishneh Torah,* recorded by Moses Maimonides. There I located the exact spot on the Mount of Olives that was described as the place for this sacrifice.

According to the Mishneh, the ceremonial burning of the red heifer happened rarely in Jewish history: the first time under Moses during the Exodus, once by Ezra, and five to seven other times after the Babylonian captivity and before the destruction of the Second Temple in AD 70. Each time, a portion of the ashes that remained from the previous sacrifice was added to the new ashes to provide spiritual continuity, creating a perpetual sacrifice. Maimonides wrote that there were only nine red heifers sacrificed from the time of the Tabernacle worship till the destruction of the Second Temple. He indicated that the tenth sacrifice of the red heifer would occur only when the messianic King was ready to appear.

The Medical Importance of the Red-Heifer Sacrifice

In addition to the obvious spiritual significance of this sacrifice, we now understand that the water of purification described in Numbers 19 actually had the ability to destroy germs and stop infection. The water of purification contained ashes of the heifer's body combined with cedar, hyssop, and scarlet thread. This water of purification contained cedar oil, which came from a type of juniper tree that grew in Israel and in the Sinai. This cedar oil would mildly irritate the skin, encouraging people to vigorously rub the water solution into their hands.

Most important, the hyssop tree — associated with mint, possibly marjoram — would produce hyssop oil, an effective antiseptic and antibacterial agent. Hyssop oil contains 50 percent carvacrol (almost identical to thymol), which is an antifungal and antibacterial agent still used in medicine, according to the book *None of These Diseases*.[16] When we note that the waters of purification were to be used to cleanse someone who had become defiled and unclean from touching a dead body, we see that this was not only a spiritual law but also an incredibly effective medical sanitation law to protect the Jews from deadly infections.

The book of Hebrews reveals that the red-heifer sacrifice had a practical medical effect. "The blood of bulls and of goats, and the ashes of an heifer sprinkling the unclean, sanctifieth to the purifying of the flesh" (Hebrews 9:13). Because of God's commands, the Jews stood apart from the pagan nations in their attention to sanitation and personal cleanliness. To fully appreciate the unusual health implications of God's commands, we need to remember that even medical doctors did not understand the need for hygiene and basic sanitation until the 1880s, when the danger of germs and infection was first discovered. The recognition of the need for sanitation and cleansing from deadly germs in the words of Scripture provide a powerful and compelling proof of the supernatural inspiration of the Word of God.

The Ashes from the Last Red-Heifer Sacrifice

The Copper Scroll, found in Cave 3 near Qumran and now located in a museum in Amman, Jordan, confirms that the last sacrifice of the ashes of the red heifer was offered just before the destruction of Jerusalem in AD 70. During the conflict, priests took the ashes from the Temple in a vessel called the *kalal,* a container made with clay and dung from a previous red heifer. The Essene priests buried the container holding the ashes near Qumran, along with a great number of other sacred objects. I am aware of several intensive archaeological investigations that seek information about the locations of the ark of the covenant, the incense from the altar, and the ashes of the red heifer. A number of investigations are being conducted under the auspices of the chief rabbis and the Israeli museums.

The chief rabbis believe the recovery of the ashes of the red heifer and the ark of the covenant are the keys to rebuilding the Temple. One group has been searching for the ashes in a cave south of Jericho for several years. And while the discovery of the ashes would be fascinating, recovering the ancient ashes from the last red-heifer sacrifice is not required by Scripture. Temple worship could resume after a ritual cleansing using ashes from the sacrifice of a new unblemished red heifer.

The Next Red-Heifer Sacrifice

For the first time in almost two thousand years, Israel is preparing to resume animal sacrifice ceremonies. However, the Temple Mount has been repeatedly defiled both by ritual impurity and the deaths of hundreds of thousands of soldiers, priests, and others during the wars of invading armies in the centuries since AD 70. These years of desecration and death have made the Temple Mount ceremonially and spiritually impure. It will be necessary to ritually and spiritually cleanse the priests, the worship vessels, and the stones of the Temple area with the waters of purification. Only then can the Sanhedrin authorize the resumption of the sacrifice system on the rebuilt altar of the Temple.

The prophet Ezekiel confirmed that the waters of purification from the red-heifer sacrifice will be used to cleanse the future Temple and the Jewish people: "Then will I sprinkle clean water upon you, and ye shall be clean: from all your filthiness, and from all your idols, will I cleanse you" (Ezekiel 36:25). He also foretold that the sacred vessels and linen robes would be prepared for use in the future Temple during the Millennium: "They shall enter into my sanctuary, and they shall come near to my table, to minister unto me, and they shall keep my charge. And it shall come to pass, that when they enter in at the gates of the inner court, they shall be clothed with linen garments; and no wool shall come upon them, while they minister in the gates of the inner court, and within" (Ezekiel 44:16–17).

This sacrifice of the red heifer symbolically pointed to Jesus Christ and His sacrifice on the cross. Our Lord, who was perfectly sinless, judicially took upon Himself the sins of the world so that we could become righteous before God. Just as the red heifer was sacrificed outside the camp in contrast to all other sacrifices that took place in front of the Tabernacle or Temple, Jesus was sacrificed outside the city of Jerusalem. In contrast to the normal practice of sacrificing only male animals, the red heifer was the only female animal the Law commanded to be sacrificed. Significantly, our Lord was betrayed for thirty pieces of silver, the price of a female slave.

An early Jewish Christian writer, Barnabas, wrote his epistle in approximately AD 120. Writing to Christians, Barnabas explained the spiritual significance of the red-heifer sacrifice as a type or symbol of Jesus Christ, who became God's sacrifice for our sins: "Now what do you suppose this to be a type of, that a command was given to Israel, that men of the greatest wickedness should offer a heifer, and slay and burn it, and . . . that the boys should sprinkle the people, one by one, in order that they might be purified from their sins? Consider how He speaks to you with simplicity. The calf is Jesus."[17]

The writer of the book of Hebrews reveals that the sacrifice of the red heifer and the resulting waters of purification symbolize the ultimate sacrifice of Jesus Christ for our sins (see Hebrews 9). Jesus Christ symbolically became sin for us during His sacrifice on the cross that we might become the righteousness of Christ when we stand before God at the judgment seat of Christ (see 2 Corinthians 5:21).

The Temple Institute has prepared more than one hundred of the sacred worship vessels and hundreds of priestly garments to be worn by Levites in future Temple services. Orthodox yeshivas, or Jewish Bible colleges, in Jerusalem have trained more than five hundred young Jewish men who are descended from the tribe of Levi to fulfill the duties of Temple worship and sacrifice. Many have been trained in worship rituals and have learned to play the recreated musical instruments such as the ancient trumpets and the lyre.

In the next chapter we will examine in detail the process of recovering and recreating sacrificial vessels and other objects that are necessary for use in Temple worship and sacrifice. Each of these objects plays a vital role in fulfilling the prophecies of the last days.

■ ■ ■ ■

SEVEN:
NEW VESSELS FOR
TEMPLE WORSHIP

RE-CREATING THE SACRED INSTRUMENTS USED IN OLD TESTAMENT SACRIFICE

■ ■ ■ ■

And let them make me a sanctuary;
that I may dwell among them.
According to all that I shew thee,
after the pattern of the tabernacle,
and the pattern of all the instruments
   thereof,
even so shall ye make it.

Exodus 25:8–9

The sanctuary contained a great variety of gold, silver, and brass vessels that were used in worship services. God gave Moses specific instructions that dictated the fashioning of the vessels to be used in daily worship in the Tabernacle (see photograph). When Solomon built the First Temple, he created a new set of vessels for the greatly expanded Temple worship services. His father, King David, had received specific instructions from the Lord for the blueprints of both the Temple and its many utensils.

The Tabernacle, the Temple, and the vessels of worship were types or symbols of the body of Jesus Christ. They illustrated the atonement for sin that He would accomplish for mankind. These objects of worship also pointed to the fulfillment of prophecy when Christ will reign from His messianic throne during the coming millennial kingdom.

More than one-third of the 613 com-

A golden crown, created for the high priest serving in the future Third Temple.

mandments that are found in the Bible and itemized in the Talmud address laws and regulations relating to the Temple. The rebuilt Temple will require a trained priesthood of Levites and Cohanim. (Cohanim are direct descendants of Aaron, the first high priest. Scientists have found a special variation of the Y chromosome that is shared by Jews descended from this priestly subtribe.)[1] Additionally, a great number of special worship vessels will need to be recreated.

Hundreds of scriptural verses command

Israel to continue with the Temple worship system forever. The prophecies of Ezekiel 40–48, Daniel 9:24–27, and Zechariah 14 predict that an Israel restored to its Promised Land will carry out the ancient Temple worship forever. In keeping with the Bible's commands, the Temple Institute was formed to research and then create more than one hundred of the sacred vessels and hundreds of priestly garments that will be needed for worship and sacrifice in the Third Temple. In this chapter we will examine the ancient treasures of the sanctuary and the plans under way to re-create these vessels.

Linen Robes for the High Priests and the Cohanim

And they made coats of fine linen of woven work for Aaron, and for his sons, and a mitre of fine linen, and goodly bonnets of fine linen, and linen breeches of fine twined linen, and a girdle of fine twined linen, and blue, and purple, and scarlet, of needlework; as the LORD commanded Moses. (Exodus 39:27–29)

Just as the Lord commanded Moses to have craftsmen create the robes for the priests, today in Jerusalem various Levites, including a young Levite woman, Yehudah

Avrasham, are weaving the garments that the hundreds of Levite and Cohanim priests

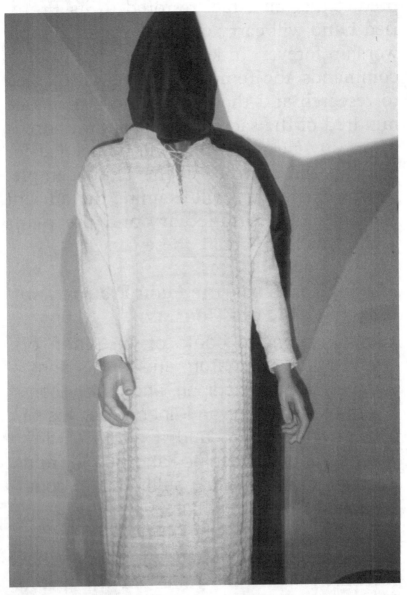

A linen garment, created by the Temple Institute for priests serving in the Third Temple.

will be required to wear while conducting worship in the Third Temple (see photograph). These robes are constructed from special six-ply linen thread. The sash is more than fifty-five feet long.

The Breastplate of the High Priest

One of the most unusual objects in ancient Israel was the breastplate of the high priest, which was made of a plate of heavy gold and twelve precious stones. This valuable item was lost when the Second Temple was burned in AD 70. The Scriptures describe that Aaron, the high priest, wore the breastplate when he served in the Tabernacle in the wilderness. Subsequent high priests wore the breastplate in their duties in the Temple.

A portion of the Copper Scroll appears to describe the place where the breastplate of the high priest was hidden two thousand years ago. The description reads as follows:

On the hill of Kohlit: tithe vessels of the Logion [the breastplate of the high priest] and the ephods. All of the tithe and of the treasure: a seventh of the second tithe from the adulterated offering. The opening is found on the shoulder of the channel coming from the north, ten cubits in the direction of the rock hewn immersion bath.[2]

As with the location of any of the hidden Temple treasures, after two thousand years it is difficult to match current topographical features with the descriptions in the Copper Scroll. In the case of the breastplate, scholars from the Temple Institute and members of the Faithful of the Temple Mount have created a replica. After much research, the twelve types of stones in the breastplate were identified and found, each of which has special characteristics.

The breastplate was constructed on a square plate of heavy gold that was a hand span high and wide (four inches approximately). According to Exodus 39:8–14, the twelve stones were set in four rows of three stones each. Each gemstone was engraved with a Hebrew letter that represented one of the twelve tribes of Israel. The top row included a sardius, a topaz, and a carbuncle. The second row was composed of an emerald, a sapphire, and a diamond. The third row included a ligure, an agate, and an amethyst. The fourth row featured a beryl, an onyx, and a jasper stone. These gemstones were enclosed in ouches (jewelry settings) of gold.

Many scholars believe the breastplate functioned with two sacred stones, the Urim and the Thummim, prophetic indicators that revealed divine answers to vital questions presented to God through the high priest. This is described in the book of Exodus:

And Aaron shall bear the names of the children of Israel in the breastplate of judgment upon his heart, when he goeth in unto the holy place, for a memorial before the LORD continually. And thou shalt put in the breastplate of judgment the Urim and the Thummim; and they shall be upon Aaron's heart, when he goeth in before the LORD: and Aaron shall bear the judgment of the children of Israel upon his heart before the LORD continually. (28:29–30)

It is intriguing to note that the book of Nehemiah states that the Urim and the Thummim on the breastplate were used to reveal the will of God regarding who was qualified to serve as Levite priests in the Second Temple after the Babylonian captivity ended in 536 BC. Nehemiah wrote, "And the Tirshatha [governor] said unto them, that they should not eat of the most holy things, till there stood up a priest with Urim and Thummim" (Nehemiah 7:65). It is reasonable to conclude from the passage in Nehemiah that Urim and Thummim will again be used to determine who is qualified to serve in the Third Temple. It appears that the phrase "Urim and Thummim" refers to the breastplate and its twelve jewels while it supernaturally revealed the Lord's will to the high priest. Some rabbis have suggested that individual stones may have "lit up" and thus indicated a specific answer to a question.

THE MIZRAK

The *mizrak* was one of the most unusual of the Temple vessels in that it was used to capture the blood from sacrificed animals. Then the blood was poured into the hollow horns at the four corners of the altar. During the regular festival days, a gold mizrak was used for this purpose. However, on the most holy day of the year, Yom Kippur, the Day of Atonement, the priest would use a large silver mizrak, weighing seventy sacred shekels — more than eight pounds of solid silver.

This mizrak was pointed on the bottom to prevent the priest from setting the vessel down prior to completing his assigned task.

According to the custom, the blood must be freshly applied to the horns of the altar and must never be allowed to congeal. This detail reminds each of us of the spiritual reality that daily we need to apply the atoning blood of Christ to our hearts.

THE ALTAR OF BURNT OFFERING

This beautiful altar stood in the courtyard in front of the sanctuary. The priest would offer an animal without blemish to be sacrificed for the sins of the people. By participating in the offering of sacrifice, the people were acknowledging their sin and asking God to cover their sins, as demanded by the Law of Moses. This sacrifice was a type or symbol of Jesus in His role as the Messiah-Redeemer. John the Baptist, when Christ approached him at the Jordan River, declared the identity and purpose of the life of Jesus Christ: "Behold the Lamb of God, which taketh away the sin of the world" (John 1:29).

The first altar of burnt offering for the Tabernacle in the wilderness was cast by Aholiab, the son of Ahisamach, of the tribe of Dan. Aholiab was given supernatural wisdom to craft the vessels for the Tabernacle. The second altar of burnt offering, built for Solomon's Temple, was cast by a

An illustration depicting a variety of Temple vessels and objects used in worship in the First and Second Temples. **Illustration c. 1890, from Blackie & Son publishers, Glasgow, Scotland**

craftsman supplied by Hiram, king of Tyre: "In the plain of Jordan did the king cast them, in the clay ground between Succoth and Zarthan" (1 Kings 7:46).

The Jews returned from Babylon in 536 BC and immediately built the altar for sacrifice prior to rebuilding the Temple. When the Third Temple is built in Jerusalem, the Levites will be prepared to begin sacrificing on a rebuilt altar prior to the actual Temple construction.

THE TABLE OF SHEWBREAD

God commanded Moses to "make a table of shittim wood: two cubits shall be the length thereof, and a cubit the breadth thereof, and a cubit and a half the height thereof (see illustration). And thou shall overlay it with pure gold, and make thereto a crown of gold round about" (Exodus 25:23–24). The bread for the offering of shewbread was placed each week by the Levites on this table as a sacrifice to the Lord. It acknowledged that God was Lord of the harvest and the source for all of the sustenance of life. The Jewish sages state that one of the miracles of the Temple was that the bread supernaturally remained fresh all week due to the Divine Presence.

The table's dimensions were three feet by

eighteen inches by twenty-seven inches. It had a five-inch-high golden crown border on the top and four gold rings at the corners to enable priests to carry it like the ark on wooden staves overlaid with gold. In preparation for the Third Temple, a re-creation of the table of shewbread was completed by the Temple Institute in the 1990s.

The bread of the table of shewbread represents in type the ultimate offering of the body of Christ, which would be broken for us. As Jesus said of the bread on the night of the Last Supper: "Take, eat; this is my body" (Matthew 26:26).

THE LAVER OF CLEANSING

Thou shalt also make a laver of brass, and his foot also of brass, to wash withal: and thou shalt put it between the tabernacle of the congregation and the altar, and thou shalt put water therein. For Aaron and his sons shall wash their hands and feet thereat. (Exodus 30:18–19)

This cleansing laver was a brass vessel that held water used to clean the hands and feet of the priests as they officiated during Temple sacrifices. Naturally, their duties involved much handling of live and dead animals, before and after each sacrifice.

Thus it was essential that they constantly clean their hands and feet so that they would remain sanctified for Temple service.

This laver of washing speaks to Christians today of the need for us to continually be washed and purified by the everlasting water of life from the Word of God, which Jesus came to provide to all who believe in and follow Him. In Ephesians 5:26–27, Paul talks of Christ's sacrifice of Himself for the church: "That he might sanctify and cleanse it with the washing of water by the word, that he might present it to himself a glorious church, not having spot, or wrinkle, or any such thing; but that it should be holy and without blemish." Here we notice that it is not enduring tribulations that sanctify and purify the bride of Christ, the church, but rather it is the washing and sanctifying process of the daily spiritual cleansing by the Word. Just as the priests of the Old Testament were purified by the waters of the laver, we are daily purified by submitting ourselves and our conduct to the cleansing action of the Word of God.

A fundamental truth of our spiritual life is that sinful conduct and the Word of God are mutually antagonistic. If a Christian finds himself involved in sin, he will usually neglect the reading of the Word. However, if, when tempted, he turns to the cleansing work of the Scriptures, he will find that as long as he focuses on the truth of God's words, sin and even its temptation will often flee from his life.

The Jerusalem Temple Institute has already reconstructed the laver of cleansing for the washing of the hands and feet of the priests. It is built of copper and brass with six faucets.

The Golden Candlestick

And thou shalt make a candlestick of pure gold: of beaten work shall the candlestick be made: his shaft, and his branches, his bowls, his knops [knobs], and his flowers, shall be of the same. And six branches shall come out of the sides of it; three branches of the candlestick out of the one side, and three branches of the candlestick out of the other. . . . And thou shalt make the seven lamps thereof. . . . Of a talent of pure gold shall he make it, with all these vessels. And look that thou make them after their pattern, which was shewed thee in the mount. (Exodus 25:31–32, 37, 39–40)

The candlestick represented to Israel the divine light of God that manifested its pres-

A golden menorah, re-created by the Temple Institute for use in the Third Temple.

ence in the Tabernacle and the Temple through the seven lamps. The light of these lamps symbolizes God's perfection. God continually uses the image of light and darkness to illustrate the light of His truth against the darkness of our sinfulness. The candlestick is a type of Christ, whom John announced as "the true Light, which lighteth every man that cometh into the world" (John 1:9). He also states of Jesus, "In him was life; and the life was the light of men" (John 1:4).

The golden candlestick, or menorah, was lost when the Roman armies captured the Second Temple. It was taken to Rome along with captives from Israel. This event was recorded in a famous bas-relief sculpture on the Arch of Titus in Rome, which commemorated the Roman victory over Jerusalem. The Levites and the Temple Institute have re-created the first of these menorahs by casting a pure bronze candelabrum seven feet high, weighing hundreds of pounds. A new, seven-branched candelabrum has also been constructed in pure gold at an estimated cost of more than $250,000 (see photograph).

THE ALTAR OF INCENSE

And thou shalt make an altar to burn incense upon: of shittim wood shalt thou make it. A cubit shall be the length thereof, and a cubit the breadth thereof; foursquare shall it be. (Exodus 30:1–2)

The altar of incense was to be placed just outside the six-inch-thick veil that hid the ark of the covenant in the Holy of Holies. Every morning and evening the high priest burned sweet incense to God when he came in to light the lamps of the candelabrum. God commanded that this incense should be burned as a "perpetual incense before the LORD throughout your generations" (Exodus 30:8).

The incense created the most wonderful fragrance, which filled the whole of Jerusalem with the aroma of worship. There is a rabbinic tradition that the incense rose straight up in the air. The cloud of perfume from the Temple incense permeated the city of Jerusalem with such a fragrance that women never needed to wear perfume, according to another tradition of the rabbis. The beautiful fragrance of the Temple incense is a type of the wonderful, sweet-smelling savor of Christ's Holy Spirit, whose presence fills our surrendered lives and makes them acceptable to our Father in heaven.

In the book of Revelation, John refers to the four living creatures that surround the throne of God, together with the twenty-four elders with harps and golden vials of incense, "which are the prayers of saints" (5:8). Our prayers are symbolized as fragrant incense as they rise to heaven's throne.

Eleven special incenses were developed according to the instructions from the Lord to Moses. A copper tray, known as the *kaf,* and a silver chalice, known as the *bazikh,* were used to carry the incense into the sacred precincts of the Temple. Additionally, a silver ring, known as a *mitultelet,* and a cloth covering were used in the daily service. All of these items have been re-created. The silver chalice holds approximately a half pound of incense, which will be sprinkled over the golden altar of incense.

The altar of incense is currently being produced by Jewish craftsmen after months of dedicated study of the Torah and the Talmudic references.

THE SILVER TRUMPETS

The Arch of Titus in Rome shows a bas-relief sculpture of the Jewish captives carrying a table with crossed silver trumpets. The Temple Institute sent technicians to Rome to carefully measure this representation of the ancient trumpets of the Temple. They reconstructed the thirty-six-inch-long sterling silver trumpets, inlaid with precious gold, exactly as found on the Arch. The Mishneh records that up to two hundred silver trumpets were used in festivals in the Temple. In Numbers 10:2 the Lord commanded Moses to make two silver trumpets for the "calling of the assembly" and the "journeying of the camps."

THE ARK OF THE COVENANT

And Bezaleel made the ark of shittim wood: two cubits and a half was the length of it, and a cubit and a half the breadth of it, and a cubit and a half the height of it: and he overlaid it with pure gold within and without, and made a crown of gold to it round about. (Exodus 37:1–2)

In the book of Revelation, John is taken in a vision to heaven, where he sees the ark of the testimony (11:19). Some have wondered if John's vision means that somehow God took the earthly ark to heaven after it disappeared from Solomon's Temple. However, we know from Exodus 25:8–10 and Exodus 25:40 that there has always been a heavenly ark of the covenant, even during the time the earthly ark was in the Tabernacle and Solomon's Temple. So there is no contradiction with the possibility that the Lord has preserved the earthly ark of the covenant on earth to be used in the Third Temple.

The ark was the physical focus of the Divine Presence. In Exodus, God states, "And there I will meet with thee, and I will commune with thee from above the mercy seat, from between the two cherubims which are upon the ark of the testimony, of all things which I will give thee in commandment unto the children of Israel" (25:22). Unlike all the other precious vessels, the ark was described as the place where God's Divine Presence would dwell continually.

The ark was forty-five inches by twenty-seven inches by twenty-seven inches, composed of acacia (shittim) wood and covered inside and out with pure gold. It was carried by means of four rings and two gold-covered wooden staves that fit through the rings to allow Levites to carry the ark on their shoulders without touching it directly. When King David and the Levites began to move the ark to Jerusalem, they forgot to obey the strict command of God regarding the procedure for carrying the ark with staves. Instead, they placed the ark on an oxcart for convenience. When the oxen stumbled and the ark began to tilt, a Levite named Uzzah attempted to keep it from falling by putting his hand on the side of the ark. Because he violated the strict law of God, Uzzah died. As a Levite priest whose family was chosen to guard the ark, Uzzah certainly knew that using the cart violated God's command. King David was so distressed that he ordered the ark taken to the house of Obededom the Gittite. After three months had passed in which Obededom and his household were tremendously blessed by God, David decided to once more bring the ark up to Jerusalem, only this time by using the staves as God had commanded (see 2 Samuel 6:1–18).

In battles such as Jericho, the Lord devastated Israel's enemies while the Jewish army carried the ark with the Divine Glory before them, terrifying the surrounding nations. When the children of Israel approached the Jordan River after wandering for forty years in the wilderness, the Levites carried the ark before them as they entered the waters. The waters of the Jordan stopped flowing and backed up miraculously to allow the Israelites to walk across on dry land.

When the ark was placed in the Holy of Holies, it was parallel to the veil and the staves of the ark were partially withdrawn toward the curtain to cause their ends to press into the veil. Thus, the priests could see that the ark was present behind the curtain, even though no one but the high priest could go behind the curtain to view it. It is recorded: "And they drew out the staves, that the ends of the staves were seen out in the holy place before the oracle, and they were not seen without: and there they are unto this day" (1 Kings 8:8).

The Mercy Seat of the Ark

And thou shalt make a mercy seat of pure gold. (Exodus 25:17)

This was the place where the Shekinah Glory dwelt. In addition to the mercy seat, which covered the top of the ark, craftsmen made two beautiful cherubim (angelic beings) of beaten gold facing each other and fixed to the mercy seat (see Exodus 25:20).

The mercy seat was the resting place for God's Shekinah Glory. The contents of the ark included the two stone tablets of the testimony (the Ten Commandments), the rod of Aaron, and a pot of manna (the food God provided supernaturally during the forty years of desert wanderings during the Exodus). However, four centuries later, at the time of King Solomon and the erecting of the First Temple, "there was nothing in the ark save the two tables of stone, which Moses put there at Horeb, when the LORD made a covenant with the children of Israel" (1 Kings 8:9).

The ark of the covenant disappeared more than three thousand years ago, during the reign of Solomon. A number of intriguing prophecies, including Isaiah 18, Jeremiah 3:15–16, and Zephaniah 3:9–10, suggest that the ark will be returned to Israel and will play a key role in the Third Temple in the last days. Despite the tremendous research and the numerous Temple vessels that are being reconstructed, all those involved with the Temple project whom I have interviewed concur that the ark of the covenant would never be rebuilt. They all believe that the ark still exists either in Ethiopia or in a chamber beneath the Temple Mount, waiting to be revealed at the moment of God's choosing.

The prophet Jeremiah suggested that when the Messiah returns, Israel will stop visiting and talking about the ark of the covenant: "And it shall come to pass, when ye be multiplied and increased in the land, in those days, saith the LORD, they shall say no more, The ark of the covenant of the LORD: neither shall it come to mind: neither shall they remember it; neither shall they visit it; neither shall that be done any more" (Jeremiah 3:16). This prophecy strongly suggests that at some point just prior to Christ's return, the ark will be restored to Israel and will be a focus of the daily Temple worship. But once Jesus rules from the throne of David in Jerusalem, the ark will no longer be the major focus of worship, as Christ will rule directly as Messiah and King of kings.

God's covenant, represented by the tablets of the Law and the ark of the covenant, promised that someday the Messiah will redeem the earth from the curse of sin and establish His millennial kingdom. Significantly, Isaiah prophesied that God will ask Israel, "Where is the house that ye build unto me?" In Isaiah 66 we find a distinct prophecy of Israel's rebirth: "Shall a nation be born at once?" (66:8). "Thus saith the LORD, The heaven is my throne, and the earth is my footstool: where is the house that ye build unto me? and where is the place of my rest?" (66:1).

If the ark is found, it would provide unprecedented motivation for the Jews to rebuild the Temple. The rediscovery of the ark also would be a rallying cry for Jews in other countries to return to the Holy Land. It would be a guarantee and reminder of God's continued covenant relationship. In the last days, the Antichrist will find the ark a tremendous temptation to capture and use as a prop for his own political and religious goals. After his initial victories over his enemies, "then shall he [Antichrist] return into his land with great riches; and his heart shall be against the holy covenant; and he shall do exploits, and return to his own land" (Daniel 11:28). While the primary fulfillment of this prophecy related to the Syrian tyrant King Antiochus IV in 168 BC, a secondary fulfillment may point to the future Antichrist's defilement of the Third Temple, an act referred to as the abomination of desolation by Daniel and Jesus. The Antichrist will hate the ark of the covenant because it is the symbol of God's unbreakable relationship with Israel.

The Divine Presence

The LORD is in his holy temple. (Psalm 11:4)

The greatest glory and treasure of the Temple was the Divine Presence, which dwelt above the ark in the Holy of Holies. When Solomon dedicated the Temple, he prayed that God's blessing and presence would always dwell at the Temple site. He also prayed that, even if Israel went into captivity, God would listen to the prayers of His people when those prayers were directed toward the Temple Mount.

In the next chapter we will examine traditions, history, legends, and eyewitness claims related to the current location of the ark of the covenant. We also will look at some reports that the ark has secretly been returned to Israel and is in safekeeping until the day when the Third Temple is completed. At that time the ark can once again be returned to the Holy of Holies.

■ ■ ■ ■

EIGHT:
THE ARK OF THE
COVENANT AND THE
THIRD TEMPLE

RELIABLE REPORTS ON THE
LOCATION OF THE ARK

■ ■ ■ ■

According to all that I shew thee, . . .
even so shall ye make it.
And they shall make an ark of shittim
   wood.

Exodus 25:9–10

Biblical commentators, including Dr. David Allen Lewis, the well-known prophecy scholar, and Arthur Bloomfield, author of *Where Is the Ark of the Covenant?* have identified the scriptural indications that the ark will return to the Temple Mount in the last days. Based on the prophecies of the Bible, they believe the ark of the covenant, after being hidden for almost three thousand years, will command headlines as it takes its place on the front lines of world events.[1]

During the first year of Israel's exodus, God directed Moses to create the Tabernacle and to construct a number of sacred objects, patterned after the worship objects in the heavenly Temple. Three of these were placed in the ark of the covenant. The first was the rod used by Aaron. As high priest, Aaron had used this rod to perform miracles before the Pharaoh of Egypt. Also placed in the ark was manna, the daily bread from

A model of the ark of the covenant.

heaven that God supernaturally provided for forty years in the Sinai wilderness. The third item was the two tablets of stone on which God had written the Ten Commandments. Aaron's rod symbolized God's sovereign choice of Israel and the supernatural deliverance from Egypt. The bowl of manna symbolized God's daily provision for His people. The tablets represented God's concern for His people, as He gave them His Law to guide them. These objects represented God's presence in the life of Israel and prophetically pointed to our salvation in Jesus Christ.

The word *ark* comes from the Hebrew word meaning a "chest, box, or coffin" (see photograph). The ark of the covenant was built of acacia wood covered with gold within and without, and its dimensions were forty-five inches by twenty-seven inches by twenty-seven inches. Atop the ark sat a pure gold lid, called the mercy seat. Two gold cherubim on top of the mercy seat represented the angelic cherubim that surround the throne of God in heaven. The Lord said that His Divine Presence, His Shekinah Glory, would dwell with the ark (see Exodus 25:22).

The ark of the covenant was placed in the Tabernacle, the tent of worship that was moved from place to place at God's command as Israel wandered through the wilderness. The priests carried the ark through the miraculously dried-up bed of the Jordan River into the Promised Land on the tenth day of the month Nisan (see Joshua 3:17; 4:19). In the famous battle of Jericho that followed, the priests carried the ark around the ancient city once a day for six days. On the seventh day they carried the ark around the city seven times and blew the trumpets according to God's command, and the walls miraculously fell, allowing the Israelites to march over the collapsed walls into the city.

(Archaeologists working from 1930 to 1936 discovered that the walls of Jericho had collapsed just as the book of Joshua records.) For centuries after that, the Israelites carried the ark into battle, gaining victories against the pagan armies that opposed them.

God gave instructions to Moses regarding the proper handling and care of the ark by the Levites (see Numbers 4:15). The holiness and Divine Presence of God that surrounded the ark was so overpowering that improper handling of it resulted in instant death. The Lord commanded that only the Levites should carry the ark and only by resting on their shoulders the poles that extended through the rings at the corners of the ark. On one occasion after the ark was returned from the Philistines, the Jewish men of Bethshemesh, out of curiosity, violated its divine sanctity by opening the lid. This caused more than fifty thousand people to die (see 1 Samuel 6:19).

When the first Temple was completed under King Solomon (approximately 980 BC), the ark, after residing in the movable Tabernacle for five centuries, was placed in the Holy of Holies. The Bible describes this dramatic event:

And the priests brought in the ark of the

covenant of the LORD unto his place, into the oracle of the house, to the most holy place, even under the wings of the cherubims. . . . There was nothing in the ark [at this time] save the two tables of stone, which Moses put there at Horeb, when the LORD made a covenant with the children of Israel, when they came out of the land of Egypt. And it came to pass, when the priests were come out of the holy place, that the cloud filled the house of the LORD, so that the priests could not stand to minister because of the cloud: for the glory of the LORD had filled the house of the LORD.

Then spake Solomon, The LORD said that he would dwell in the thick darkness. I have surely built thee an house to dwell in, a settled place for thee to abide in for ever. (1 Kings 8:6, 9–13)

God's Shekinah Glory dwelt on the mercy seat and guided and protected Israel. It symbolized the person of Christ, the Messiah, who would fulfill God's covenant with His people.

The ark remained in the Temple until the final years of King Solomon's reign when, according to many scholars, it was taken to Ethiopia. From the time of Solomon till the present, the Bible is strangely silent about the location of the ark. We know it was not present in the Temple after the Jewish captives returned from Babylon in 536 BC. Yet according to the prophet Jeremiah, the ark of the covenant will play a pivotal role in the future. He prophesied that, just before the return of the Messiah, Israel will once again visit and talk about the ark (see Jeremiah 3:16–17). When the Messiah comes, the ark will no longer be the central focus of Israel's worship; they will then worship Christ directly. This prophecy implies that this sacred object must play a crucial role in the prophetic events leading up to the building of the Third Temple, the defilement of the Temple by the Antichrist, and the coming of the Messiah.

THE SEARCH FOR THE ARK

The movie *Raiders of the Lost Ark* was based on a real search for the lost ark of the covenant just before World War II. The film shows a fictional archaeologist, Indiana Jones, hunting for the ark in 1936. The movie tells of the Nazis' fascination with the ark and other sacred objects and of their search for the ark in Egypt. In fact, both the German Nazis and the Italian Fascists, led by dictator Benito Mussolini, were intrigued by the ark of the covenant. Historical records indicate that one of the war aims of the Italian army that invaded Ethiopia in 1935 was to capture the ark.

Amid the ongoing fascination with the ark, two questions remain: What happened to the holy ark in the first place, and where is it now?

In his detailed prophecy describing the supernatural victory over the coming Russian-Arab invasion of Israel in the War of Gog and Magog, Ezekiel recorded the Lord's words: "I will set my glory among the heathen, and all the heathen shall see my judgment that I have executed, and my hand that I have laid upon them. So the house of Israel shall know that I am the LORD their God from that day and forward" (Ezekiel 39:21–22). Throughout the Scriptures the phrase "my glory" is used exclusively in reference to either Christ or to the Shekinah Glory surrounding the ark of the covenant. The words "I will set my glory among the heathen" may refer to the actual presence of God's glory above the mercy seat of the ark. This prophecy may indicate that the lost ark will be brought forth during this supernatural defeat of Israel's enemies in the near future.

To discover the truth about the ark of the covenant, we will need to examine evidence from two different sources: (1) the secular history of ancient Ethiopia and (2) the prophecies and historical records of the Bible. The last time the ark was unquestionably in the hands of Israel is reported in 2 Chronicles 8:11, in which Solomon asked his wife, the pagan daughter of the Egyptian Pharaoh, to leave the area where the ark was stored because she was not a Jewish believer. Shortly after that event, the ark disappeared from Israel's national life. In all of the Bible's subsequent accounts of battles, rebellions, invasions, and looting of the Temple by various pagan empires, the Scriptures are silent about the ark's location.

WAS THE ARK MOVED TO ETHIOPIA?

The queen of Sheba visited King Solomon several years after he placed the ark of the covenant in the Holy of Holies. Second Chronicles 9:12 tells us, "And king Solomon gave to the queen of Sheba all her desire, whatsoever she asked, beside that which she had brought unto the king. So she turned, and went away to her own land, she and her servants." We know that Solomon was not averse to female companionship, marrying foreign women, or having children by them. According to Ethiopian history, the queen of Sheba married King Solomon, and they produced a royal heir. According to the Ethiopian Royal Chronicles, Prince Menelik I was born from their union. He grew up in the palace in Jerusalem. While being educated by the priests of the Temple, he became a strong believer in Jehovah.

In 1935 Leo Roberts wrote an article published in *National Geographic* that recorded his interviews with various priests in different parts of Ethiopia, all of whom told the following story. "Solomon educated the lad in Jerusalem until he was nineteen years old. The boy then returned to Ethiopia with a large group of Jews, taking with him the true ark of the covenant. Many people believe that this ark is now in some church along the northern boundary of present-day Ethiopia, near Aduwa (Adua) or Aksum."[2] Roberts made it clear that the ark, if it was in fact in Ethiopia, was so well guarded that no Western researcher had been able to verify the legend.

This same ancient tradition also appears in an article in the *Encyclopaedia Britannica Online:* "Aksum has long been regarded a holy city for the Ethiopian Orthodox church. It forms the setting of the 14th-century work *Kebra Negast* [The Glory of the Kings, the Ethiopian royal historical records], which relates the tradition of the transference of the ark of the covenant from Jerusalem to Aksum by King Menilek I, legendary son of Solomon and the Queen of Sheba (Makeda)."[3] The article identifies the traditional location of the ark as the Church of St. Mary of Zion.

Several detailed Ethiopian murals tell how the ark and the tablets of the Law were taken to Ethiopia for safekeeping by Prince Menelik I. The records indicate that when the queen of Sheba died, her nineteen-year-old son prepared to leave Jerusalem to return to his native country to become its king. Before Menelik I left Israel, Solomon (to whom the prince bore an uncanny resemblance) ordered his craftsmen to create a perfect replica of the ark for his son to take to Ethiopia. The great distance (2,500 miles) would prevent the prince from ever again worshiping at the Temple in Jerusalem.

However, the question arises: which ark did the prince take to Ethiopia, the true ark or the replica? Ethiopian records suggest that Prince Menelik was very concerned with the growing apostasy of Israel and the fact that his father, Solomon, was allowing pagan idols to be placed in the Temple to please his pagan wives. Solomon gave the prince a going-away banquet and, after the priests were filled with wine, Menelik and some associates switched the replica ark with the true ark. The royal archives record that Menelik and a group of Jewish priests, along with representatives from most of the twelve tribes of Israel, removed the true ark of the covenant to Ethiopia for safekeeping until Israel repented of its idol worship. Ethiopian records claim that Menelik left the perfect replica in the Holy of Holies of the First Temple. Only he and his conspirators knew of the substitution.

Unfortunately, in the course of the last three thousand years, Israel has never repented as a nation or returned to the laws of the Scriptures. As a result, Israel suffered a succession of mostly evil kings until the Assyrians conquered Israel in 722 BC and the Babylonians conquered Judah in 586 BC. Thus, the Jewish descendants of Menelik I of Ethiopia, the royal son of Solomon, never returned the ark to Jerusalem. The descendants of Menelik I and his Jewish priests, advisors, and servants from the various tribes of Israel called themselves House of Israel. Today they are known as

Falasha Jews.

The Ethiopian descendants of Israel formed the ruling class during thousands of years of Ethiopian history. The royal dynasty from Solomon and the queen of Sheba ruled continuously until the twelfth century. The Ethiopian royal chronicles record that the Jewish Ethiopian kingdom was ruled by Queen Judith around AD 950, and the dynasty continued for another two centuries. For several hundred years following a Muslim invasion in the twelfth century, Muslims ruled most of Ethiopia until the original Solomonic dynasty was reestablished in 1558 by a Jewish king. That Ethiopian Jewish dynasty continued until the communist coup in 1974 and the death of Emperor Haile Selassie (who called himself the "Lion of Judah") in 1975.

The prophet Zephaniah (3:10) predicted that in the last days, the Jews of Ethiopia would return to Israel from their three-thousand-year exile. After a great deal of research, debate, and counsel, the two chief rabbis of Israel accepted the Falasha, the Ethiopian Jews, as legitimate Jews who were separated from the twelve tribes in the ancient past. Over the last fifty years, thousands of Ethiopian Jews have trickled back to Israel. However, Israel only officially admitted the Falashas into Israel under the Law of Return as legitimate Jews beginning in 1989. Tens of thousands of the Falasha have since returned to the Promised Land.

SIGNS OF THE ARK IN ETHIOPIA

Visitors to Ethiopia have reported that the altars and communion tables of both ancient and modern Christian churches there contain a carving of the ark of the covenant, called the *tabot* (the "Holy Ark"), which represents the ancient ark in Aksum. Several news articles also have mentioned Ethiopia as a likely location of the ark. The Jewish magazine *B'nai B'rith Messenger* reported the following in 1935:

The Tablets of the Law received by Moses on Mount Sinai and the Ark of the Covenant, are both said to have been brought to Ethiopia from Jerusalem by Menelik. . . . During the mid 1930's the Ark and the Tablets were removed to the [Ethiopian] mountain strongholds of Abyssinia for safekeeping because of the impending Italian invasion.[4]

In 1981 Canada's largest newspaper, the *Toronto Star,* stated the following:

In July 1936, a news service reported . . . that a Semitic syndicate had approached French underwriters about insuring the Ark — said by the dispatch to be in Ethiopia — against war damage. The report explained that [the Ark] was carried in ancient times as a protection against the enemy. It was believed that the Ethiopians . . . might again bring it forth.[5]

Starting in 1948, the Israeli government enjoyed close relations with Emperor Haile Selassie and supplied considerable technical support and financial aid to Ethiopia. Members of the Ethiopian royal family have told me that Israeli agents repeatedly asked the emperor about the ark of the covenant. The Israelis suggested that since Israel had returned to the Holy Land and then had recaptured the Temple Mount in 1967, the time had come for the Ethiopians to return the ark to Jerusalem. My contacts report that Emperor Selassie agreed that in principle, the ark should be returned to Israel. However, he felt that the correct time had not yet come. He felt that God would reveal the right time.

Though the emperor and many members of his family were imprisoned after the communist coup, a number of his descendants escaped and are living in the West. The current emperor, Crown Prince Zera Yacob, a great-grandson of Haile Selassie, is living in exile in England. I have met many times with Prince Stephen Mengesha, another great-grandson of Haile Selassie, who lives in Canada. He agreed to several interviews in connection with my research. Mengesha's father, Prince Mengesha Seyoum, was the governor-general of Ethiopia, ruling the northern province of Tigre, which contains the ancient city of Aksum, where the ark was hidden thousands of years ago. Mengesha Seyoum was interviewed on a national religious television program *(PTL)* in the United States in the fall of 1990. In that interview he verified that the ark was in Ethiopia, saying the historic Church of St. Mary of Zion in Aksum was the repository of the ark.

The church's original building was burned during the sixteenth century. The present church was rebuilt several hundred years ago over the original foundations and sub-basements of the ancient repository. On the television program, Mengesha Seyoum showed video footage of his leading Queen Elizabeth and Prince Philip on an official visit to the church. Far beneath the ancient church a secret passage leads to a heavily guarded hiding place. For three thousand years this passage to the Ethiopian Holy of Holies has been protected by priestly guards of the Ethiopian Jewish monarchy. Within this underground temple are seven concentric rings of circular walls. An Ethiopian Coptic priest can worship within the areas of the first to the fourth outermost rings. Only the highest priests and the emperor can enter the fifth and sixth innermost rings.

The final, seventh ring forms a walled circular room. It is the Holy of Holies. The Ethiopians claim that the ark of the covenant — with the mercy seat and the Shekinah Glory of God — has been protected in this room for three thousand years. Only one person is allowed to enter — he is called the guardian of the ark. This Ethiopian priest-guard is chosen at the age of seven, the age of understanding, from the main priestly family. He is trained as a child, in his age of innocence, and agrees to guard the ark for the rest of his life. This individual chooses to forgo a normal life. The guardian fasts for 225 days every year, according to the Ethiopian Jewish sacred festival calendar. He prays, meditates, and guards the ark with his life. He leaves the Holy of Holies only upon his death, when he is replaced by another chosen guardian. Each day the high priest enters the sixth innermost ring to bring the guardian food and water.

What does the Bible say, if anything, about the location of the ark after the time of Solomon? There is one brief mention of an ark in 2 Chronicles 35:3, where King Josiah orders the priests to return the ark to the Temple. It had been removed by a wicked king to make room for pagan idols. However, it is unlikely that this ark is the true ark of the covenant, because the biblical writer does not call it the ark of the covenant. Naturally, the replica ark would be identical to the true ark, and the priests of King Josiah would have believed that the replica was the real ark of the covenant. Also, in light of the devastating divine punishment given to previous defilers of the true ark, it is difficult to believe that an evil king could have simply removed the true ark and substituted idols in its place without suffering divine retribution.

If Ethiopian history is correct, the ark object referred to in 2 Chronicles 35:3 was a replica of the true ark. This would explain how the leaders of Israel could have removed it with impunity.

And what of the ark that possibly has been sighted in a chamber deep below the Temple

221

Mount? If the Ethiopian tradition is correct, the priests in Jerusalem would have treated the replica ark as the genuine item. They would have hidden it to keep it out of the hands of the Babylonians. In other words, if there is an ark hidden underneath the Temple Mount, it may be the replica. If it were to be rediscovered and identified, it should be treated as the genuine ark. No one will be able to prove whether it is genuine unless they dare to touch it (see 2 Samuel 6:6–7).

WAS THE ARK RETURNED TO ISRAEL?

During the mid-1990s, I interviewed three individuals who had personal knowledge of a secret mission carried out at the end of the Ethiopian civil war. Two of my sources, one Ethiopian and one Israeli, knew people who participated in this mission to bring the ark back to Jerusalem. The third source was the late Honorable Robert N. Thompson, a former Canadian diplomat and former senior member of Canada's Parliament. He traveled to Ethiopia during the final days of its civil war in a successful attempt to rescue the surviving members of the Ethiopian royal family who were under arrest by the Marxist dictator. I have known Thompson as a family friend since I was a young boy and have admired his career as a military officer, a missionary, a member of Parliament, a leader of a conservative political party in Canada, and a diplomat serving as Canada's ambassador to NATO. In the years following World War II, he served as an advisor to Emperor Haile Selassie, assisting in the creation of Ethiopia's educational and health-care systems. During one of his visits to my parents' home when I was a young boy, he told me that the true ark of the covenant was hidden in Aksum. Following his return to Canada after the rescue of members of the Ethiopian royal family, I had the opportunity to speak with him again. He revealed that his Ethiopian sources had disclosed details that confirm the story I am about to relate. Every one of my three sources confirmed portions of the following account.

During the final days of the Ethiopian civil war, negotiations took place between Israeli intelligence agents and Ethiopia's Marxist generals concerning the ark of the covenant. The Ethiopian military leaders demanded a bribe of tens of millions of dollars to allow the ark to be taken to Israel. A number of wealthy Jews donated the necessary funds. Suitcases containing the ransom money were delivered to the corrupt officials, who promptly left Ethiopia at the end of the civil war to fly to Switzerland. However, unknown to the departing Marxist officials, the suitcases contained counterfeit U.S. dollars. The Israeli agents phoned the Swiss banks to inform them of the counterfeit nature of the currency. Israel then took the real money raised by Jewish donors and gave it to the neighboring Eritrean rebels who had just conquered the Ethiopian capital of Addis Ababa. Since the fleeing officials had looted the country's treasury, these funds were desperately needed by the new Ethiopian government. Since then Israel has developed excellent relations with the Ethiopian government and provides a great deal of technical support.

My sources tell me that an elite team of Israeli Special Forces flew an unmarked cargo plane into the northern province of Gonder and secretly entered the city of Aksum at night during the chaos of the closing days of the civil war. Each of the Israelis was a handpicked soldier, and each was a descendant of the tribe of Levi. According to the Law of Moses, only trained Levites were to carry the ark of the covenant (see Numbers 4:15).

Apparently secret negotiations had been held with Ethiopia's senior religious leaders as well as the surviving members of the royal family (in light of Emperor Selassie's earlier agreement that the ark should return to Israel). The special troops removed the ark from the underground treasury beneath the Church of Saint Mary of Zion. The Levites carried the ark, with its special blue covering, into a military cargo plane using staves to hoist it on their shoulders, in the biblically prescribed manner. After arriving in Israel, the ark was taken to a secure location near Jerusalem, where it will be held until the time comes to place it within the Holy of Holies of the Third Temple. My sources tell me that a replica of the ark of the covenant was placed in the Ethiopian Holy of Holies in Aksum, thus repeating history.

A report such as this is impossible to document independently. However, the three people who gave me this information are very credible, and the facts related are consistent with other details I have discovered on my own. Many Orthodox rabbis believe the ark of the covenant is now back in Israel in a secret vault until God gives the signal to rebuild the Temple.

Another Theory:
Was the Ark Always in Jerusalem?

If the ark was not in fact transported to Ethiopia during the final years of the reign of King Solomon, another possibility is that the ark was hidden underneath the Temple Mount to protect it from the invading Babylonian armies, as rabbinic tradition states. Some Jewish writers have suggested that the ark is in one of the secret tunnels underneath the Temple Mount.

This hiding place was under the continuous control of Israel's enemies from the fall of Jerusalem in AD 70 until the Six-Day War in 1967. Since 1967 Jewish archaeologists have explored many of the subterranean structures beneath the Temple Mount. This work proceeded under the direction of the late chief rabbi Shlomo Goren and the late chief rabbi of the Western Wall, Rabbi Yehuda Getz. Teams of researchers explored secret tunnels and chambers far beneath the surface of the thirty-five-acre Temple enclosure. One of their goals was to determine the location of the treasures of the Temple (including the ark), which they believe priests buried during the two-year siege before the city finally fell to the Roman army in AD 70.

On May 15, 1992, the CBS television network broadcast a two-hour special called "Ancient Secrets of the Bible." One of the topics covered was the location of the ark of the covenant. The narrator claimed that Rabbi Getz discovered the ark of the covenant under the Temple Mount. My source (who was also a member of the initial investigating team) told me they did not have an opportunity to closely examine the object in question. In fear of violating the sacred area of the ancient Holy of Holies, they held back from entering the tunnel. So they were able to see it only through the illumination of their flashlights at a distance of some fifty feet. The conclusion of Rabbis Getz and Goren was that they had *probably* seen the ark. Unfortunately, Arabs broke through the tunnel from overhead, through the Dome of the Rock substructures, and prevented the researchers from examining the object. Within hours the Arabs used concrete to seal the opening into the tunnel. This prevented further Jewish exploration, and at this point we can't be certain if the object sighted was the true ark of the covenant. I would presume that the object may either be the replica of the ark that was made for Prince Menelik I or possibly another sacred object from the Temple, such as the altar of incense.

CBS Television asked me to participate in the program with my research and unique film of the Temple Mount tunnels, as well as the evidence that suggests the ark had been taken to Ethiopia. Our film crew's video of the secret tunnels and Temple treasuries was shown to illustrate the ongoing exploration effort. During the program I explained the history of the ark and the evidence that it has been guarded in an underground chamber in Ethiopia, where it has been stored for thousands of years.

No matter where the true ark is currently located, the Bible indicates that it has a significant prophetic role to play in the final events of this age. Only future events will reveal the truth about the location of the hidden ark of the covenant.

THE ARK'S PROPHETIC ROLE

Do biblical prophecies reveal anything about the location of the ark of the covenant? In Isaiah 18 we find the clearest indication that the ark will be brought from Ethiopia in the end times. God addresses the people of Ethiopia in the first two verses of Isaiah 18 and tells them of the role they will play in the events of the last days. Isaiah's prophecy reads, "Woe to the land shadowing with wings, which is beyond the rivers of Ethiopia. . . . All ye inhabitants of the world, and dwellers on the earth, see ye, when he lifteth up an ensign [*nes*, ark] on the mountains; and when he bloweth a trumpet, hear ye." The closing verse declares, "In that time shall the present [*nes*, ark] be brought unto the LORD of hosts . . . [from Ethiopia] . . . to the place of the name of the LORD of hosts, the mount Zion" (18:1, 3, 7). This prophecy may refer to an already-accomplished development — the return of the ark from Ethiopia in the early 1990s.

Another fascinating prophecy, this one by Zephaniah, states that Israel will miraculously have its language, Hebrew, restored to it when God brings the Jews back into their land: "For then will I turn to the people a pure language, that they may all call upon the name of the LORD, to serve him with one consent. From beyond the rivers of Ethiopia my suppliants, even the daughter of my dispersed, shall bring mine offering" (Zephaniah 3:9–10). Even in the time of Christ, Hebrew was a dying language. It was used only by the scribes and priests for official religious purposes in the Temple. Almost everyone else used the Greek language, which had become the "international" language of its day. Many conversations would be in Aramaic, a language the Jewish exiles adopted during their seventy years of captivity in Babylon. The revival of the ancient language of Hebrew in modern Israel is another miraculous and unprecedented fulfillment of prophecy in our day. This recovery of a dead language and its revival after some two thousand years is a phenomenon without historical precedent.

Notice that the passage in Isaiah 18 connects the time of the return of the "present" to the rebirth of Israel and the time of the revival of the Hebrew language (see Zephaniah 3:9–10). This "present" may very well be the return of the lost ark of the covenant.

One final prophecy provides, perhaps, the strongest evidence that the ark will be recovered and play an important role in our future. Jeremiah describes a time after the battle of Armageddon has been won and Israel is enjoying its messianic kingdom:

And it shall come to pass, when ye be multiplied and increased in the land, in those days, saith the LORD, they shall say no more, The ark of the covenant of the LORD: neither shall it come to mind:

neither shall they remember it; neither shall they visit it; neither shall that be done any more. At that time they shall call Jerusalem the throne of the LORD; and all the nations shall be gathered unto it, to the name of the LORD, to Jerusalem. (Jeremiah 3:16–17)

In other words, Jeremiah prophesied that once the battle of Armageddon is over and the millennial kingdom has commenced, Israel will stop talking about the ark, stop thinking about the ark, and stop visiting the ark. The reason the ark of the covenant will no longer be as important is that Jesus will be present to be worshiped directly as the Messiah-King.

However, this prophecy of Jeremiah does not make sense unless the lost ark is rediscovered and unless, in the years leading up to Israel's final great crisis, the ark plays a pivotal role in the spiritual life of the nation. Obviously, if the ark was to be publicly revealed and brought to the newly built Third Temple, the ark would be talked about, thought about, and visited.

The return of the ark of the covenant to the Holy of Holies of a rebuilt Temple would signal for Israel the final ushering in of the messianic era. Only time will reveal the true role of the ark of the covenant in the events that will surround the rise of the Antichrist and the return of Jesus as Israel's Messiah.

■ ■ ■ ■

NINE:
PREPARING FOR THE
COMING MESSIAH

THE EVENTS OF THE LAST DAYS
ARE UPON US

■ ■ ■ ■

I will make a covenant of peace with them;
it shall be an everlasting covenant with
   them:
and I will place them, and multiply them,
and will set my sanctuary in the midst of
   them
for evermore.

Ezekiel 37:26

Ezekiel foretold the miraculous rebirth of Israel and the future rebuilding of the Temple, two events that will lead to the return of Jesus Christ to set up His millennial kingdom on earth.

Thus saith the Lord GOD; Behold, I will take the children of Israel from among the heathen, whither they be gone, and will gather them on every side, and bring them into their own land: and I will make them one nation in the land upon the mountains of Israel; and one king shall be king to them all. (Ezekiel 37:21–22)

After the destruction of Jerusalem in AD 70, Israel as a nation existed only in the hopes of future generations of Jews and in the words of prophecy. Nineteen hundred years would pass before the modern State of Israel was proclaimed an independent nation at midnight on May 14, 1948.

During the 1880s anti-Semitic persecution within Russia and Ukraine forced many Jews to flee to Palestine and North America. In 1896 Theodor Herzl wrote a pamphlet, *The Jewish State,* which aroused an intense longing to return to Zion among Jews living in exile. It is fascinating to realize that Christian Zionists who believed the biblical prophecies helped influence Herzl and other Jewish leaders to focus on Israel as their Promised Land, not on Uganda or some other available land. Another step toward the rebirth of Israel was taken at the end of World War I when the Allied powers dismembered the Turkish Empire, which had sided with Germany in the war.

In 1917 British foreign secretary Arthur Balfour wrote his famous Balfour Declaration, which favored "the establishment in Palestine of a national home for the Jewish people." The declaration specified that the establishment of a Jewish nation must not "prejudice the civil and religious rights of existing non-Jewish communities in Palestine, or the rights and political status enjoyed by Jews in any other country."[1] The Balfour agreement was endorsed on July 24, 1922, by the Council of the League of Nations (the forerunner of the United

Nations) plus fifty-two nations, including the United States, and for a short time even some Arab leaders.

Emir Faisal ibn Hussein, the leader of the Arab Kingdom, met several times with the Zionist leader, Dr. Chaim Weizmann. One of their declarations, signed in 1919, stated that "the surest means of working out the consummation of their national aspirations is through the closest possible collaboration in the development of the Arab State and Palestine [the Jewish Homeland]."[2] In 1919 Emir Faisal wrote to Zionist leader Felix Frankfurter, a U.S. Supreme Court judge, declaring, "We Arabs, especially the educated among us, look with the deepest sympathy on the Zionist movement. . . . Our two movements complete one another. The Jewish movement is national and not imperialist. Our movement is national and not imperialist, and there is room in Syria [which at that time included all of Palestine] for us both."[3]

These friendly sentiments were not shared by all Arabs and had all but died out by 1948, when Israel officially became a nation once again. Almost immediately an alliance of Arab nations invaded Israel and for more than a year Israel and the surrounding nations were at war. A peace agreement was brokered, but it would not last. In 1967, after the Arab states prepared once again to attack, Israel regained control of the Temple Mount in the Six-Day War. In 1973 the Israelis again defended their land against a surprise Arab attack during the brief Yom Kippur War. Limited attacks have marked the past thirty years, with terrorist groups such as the Palestinian Liberation Organization, Hamas, and Hezbollah launching attacks against Israeli citizens.

As we can see on any newscast today, terrorism and Middle Eastern hatred of Israel is escalating. These actions will culminate in a battle predicted in Scripture.

PROPHESIED TREASURES FROM THE DEAD SEA

Throughout the Scriptures we find numerous prophecies that refer to God placing treasures for Israel within the seas. For many centuries these predictions seemed unlikely to ever be fulfilled. However, since the rebirth of Israel, scientists and engineers have developed enormous mineral resources from the Dead Sea. The Bible includes the following prophecies:

They shall call the people unto the mountain; there they shall offer sacrifices of

238

righteousness: for they shall suck of the abundance of the seas, and of treasures hid in the sand. (Deuteronomy 33:19)

And I will give thee the treasures of darkness, and hidden riches of secret places, that thou mayest know that I, the LORD, which call thee by thy name, am the God of Israel. (Isaiah 45:3)

O thou that dwellest upon many waters, abundant in treasures, thine end is come, and the measure of thy covetousness. (Jeremiah 51:13)

In the 1930s the British Mandate authorities allowed a British company known as Potash, Ltd. to set up a pumping and extraction plant that would recover some of the extraordinary mineral wealth from the Dead Sea — wealth that had been hidden by God as "the treasures of darkness, and hidden riches of secret places" (Isaiah 45:3). The company pumped a slushlike supersaturated liquid from a depth of two hundred feet at the northern end of the Dead Sea. The liquid moved through a thirty-inch pipe some twelve hundred feet up the side of mountains to the west of the Dead Sea. The company had scraped out enormous evaporation pans near the top of a mountain. Five huge pools were arranged in a cascadelike series, with each evaporation pan spilling over to the next lower pool.

The unusually high temperatures and high winds of the area cause the slushlike material to evaporate, producing extremely pure sodium chloride (table salt, which is highly valuable). The residue was poured into the next evaporation pool and after evaporation produced magnesium chloride (used in the manufacture of aluminum). Each additional evaporation pool produced another chemical separation: calcium chloride, potassium chloride, and finally magnesium bromide. When I searched the Internet to determine

Chemical	Est. Billion Tons	Price per Ton	Total Value
Magnesium chloride	22	$290	$6.38 trillion
Sodium chloride	11	$450	$4.95 trillion
Calcium chloride	5	$350	$1.75 trillion
Potassium chloride	2	$85	$170 billion
Magnesium bromide	1	$1,280	$1.28 trillion
Total Estimate	41		Over $14 trillion

Annual addition of potassium chloride to Dead Sea: 40,000 tons* (*This amount is more than enough to replenish the annual harvest.)[4]

the current values of the amount of chemicals that have been calculated to exist in the Dead Sea, I arrived at these incredible figures (see table).

To place this $14 trillion value in perspective, it is virtually equal to the annual gross national product of the United States.

The Lord has not only brought His people back to their land, but He is motivating them to restore its ancient fertility and wealth as it was in the days of King David and King Solomon.

THE WAR OF GOG AND MAGOG

Prophetic signposts clearly indicate we are quickly approaching the final turning point — the Second Coming of Jesus Christ to set up His kingdom. Prior to that long-awaited event, a great battle will take place in which the Lord will protect Israel from a massive invading army.

An unprecedented military alliance will form, led by Russia. The alliance will be made up of Islamic nations, including virtually all Middle Eastern Arab and Islamic states, North African states, Central Asian (former southern U.S.S.R.) states, plus Iran and a number of Asian nations. In Ezekiel 38:2–6 God prophesied in great detail the names of the ancient nations that will invade

Israel. Magog is identified as Russia by both Josephus and Herodotus, ancient Jewish and Greek historians respectively. The prophecy specifically names Iran (Persia), Ethiopia, and Libya in North Africa. The names Gomer and Togarmah are believed to refer to nations of Central Asia.

The alliance will attack Israel in an overpowering attempt to annihilate the chosen people. The prophet Ezekiel declared that God will employ supernatural means to defend Israel in this war, the coming War of Gog and Magog. The Lord will intervene to destroy 85 percent of the Russian-Islamic army by means of fire and brimstone, plague, madness, and the greatest earthquake in history (see Ezekiel 38:19–22; 39:1–2, 6).

The devastation will be so vast that cities around the world will be shaken. The global earthquake will cause buildings, bridges, and walls to crumble. The Scriptures prophesy that it will take seven months just to bury the fallen soldiers, and it will take seven years for Israel to burn the weapons of the invaders. Out of this profound global crisis, a political, military, and religious transformation will occur. God says, "And they shall know that I am the Lord GOD" (Ezekiel 28:24). With Russia and its Islamic allies militarily devastated, the political-military balance of the world will be transformed.

Many Christians wonder how the United States will align itself at the time of the War of Gog and Magog. I believe we will see a major shift in American foreign policy in the near future, with America withdrawing from its role as world policeman to adopt a policy of isolationism. The massive reduction (virtually 50 percent) in the size of the U.S. military during the Clinton administration and the natural war-weariness from the continuing wars in Iraq and Afghanistan may explain why there is so little specific prophecy about America in the last days.

If this seems far-fetched, think about the radical changes that will take place in the United States after the Rapture. All born-again Christians will be instantly transferred to heaven, vacating their positions in government, education, business, the church, and the military. When the salt is removed, spiritual rot will quickly set in. As America finds itself without the Christian leadership that has been the foundation of its greatness for several centuries, the balance of geopolitical and military power will shift dramatically to Europe and the Pacific Rim nations. As the Bible prophesies, the focus of world events will turn to the Middle East, Israel, and the revived Roman Empire of Europe and North Africa.

The Scriptures prophesy that, following the supernatural defeat of the Russian and Islamic armies when they attempt to annihilate Israel, the nations of the European Union and the Middle East will step into the political-military vacuum created by the elimination of both Russia's and Islamic military power. Both Daniel and the book of Revelation contain prophecies that point to the revival of the Roman Empire as the world's next superpower (Daniel 2:40–45; 7:23–25; Revelation 13:1, 7).

We are entering a dangerous period of history. In spite of a heightened desire for peace, there is little reduction in the vast armaments available to dictators, terrorists, and rogue nations. With friendly nations withdrawing from their traditional stance of active support of American foreign policy, Europe is truly uniting for the first time since the fall of the Roman Empire more than fifteen centuries ago. A united Europe will be an economic, political, and military colossus on the transformed world stage once the prophesied global dictator rises to seize power in Europe. Each of the major players described in prophecy is moving into its appointed place to fulfill the prophecies concerning the birth pangs of the Messianic Age, the coming Great Tribulation, and the return of Christ.

We are commanded to remain alert and live each day in the awareness that Christ is coming soon:

> For when they shall say, Peace and safety; then sudden destruction cometh upon them, as travail upon a woman with child; and they shall not escape. But ye, brethren, are not in darkness, that that day should overtake you as a thief. Ye are all the children of light, and the children of the day: we are not of the night, nor of darkness. Therefore let us not sleep, as do others, but let us watch and be sober. (1 Thessalonians 5:3–6)

THE ANTICHRIST, THE ARK, AND THE TEMPLE

At some point during the lifetime of this generation, at God's appointed time, the Third Temple will be built, possibly following the War of Gog and Magog. The Holy of Holies in the Third Temple will once again house the ark of the covenant, which was the major object in the Temple that pointed clearly to the second coming of the Messiah. The ark is a profound symbol to the Jews and a guarantee of God's unbreakable covenant with Israel. The presence of the ark also will factor into the evil that will be brought about by the Antichrist during the Tribulation.

A quick overview of the seven-year Tribulation period shows that there are two distinct sections: (1) During the first half (three and a half years), the Antichrist presents himself as the messiah — an economic, political, religious, and military genius who rules globally and supports Israel. (2) To begin the second period of three and a half years, the Antichrist will stop the Temple sacrifice. He will then be assassinated, and to the wonder of all humanity, he will be satanically resurrected. He will proclaim that he is "god" and will defile the Holy of Holies. This defilement of the Temple by stopping the daily sacrifice begins the second half of the seven-year Tribulation (see Matthew 24:21). The prophet Daniel confirms that the elimination of the daily sacrifice in the Temple by the orders of the Antichrist will begin the three-and-a-half-year period (1,290 days) that will constitute the "Great Tribulation," the terrible persecution of the Antichrist under the Mark of the Beast police totalitarian control system (Daniel 12:11; Revelation 13:16–18). That three-and-a-half-year period of the Great Tribulation will end with the cataclysmic battle of Armageddon and Jesus Christ's triumphant return in glory to set up His kingdom on earth.

We know from Daniel that the Antichrist will violate his seven-year treaty with Israel after three and a half years. He will stop the daily sacrifices and enter the Holy of Holies. "He shall confirm the covenant with many for one week: and in the midst of the week he shall cause the sacrifice and the oblation to cease, and for the overspreading of abominations he shall make it desolate" (Daniel 9:27).

The apostle Paul warned about the son of perdition "who opposeth and exalteth himself above all that is called God, or that is worshipped; so that he as God sitteth in the temple of God, shewing himself that he is God" (2 Thessalonians 2:4). This prophecy will be fulfilled when the Antichrist enters the Third Temple and defiles the restored ark of the covenant, possibly by touching it or sitting on the mercy seat or worse. This would qualify as the abomination of desolation mentioned by Daniel and by Jesus (see Matthew 24:15). The Antichrist's defilement of the Holy Place is so abominable that the wrath of God will be instantly poured out on Jerusalem. Christ referred to this time: "When ye therefore shall see the abomination of desolation, spoken of by Daniel the prophet, stand in the holy place, (whoso readeth, let him understand:) then let them which be in Judaea flee into the mountains. . . . For then shall be great tribulation, such as was not since the beginning of the world to this time, no, nor ever shall be" (Matthew 24:15–16, 21).

When the Prince of Darkness defiles the Temple, many Jews will recognize that he is a false messiah. After the Antichrist defiles the Temple, someone will kill him with a sword. It may be a Jewish believer who breaks through his security and succeeds in stabbing him with a sword in the head or neck. John's description of the assassination suggests the Antichrist will succumb to a head or neck wound: "I saw one of his heads as it were wounded to death; and his deadly wound was healed: and all the world wondered after the beast" (Revelation 13:3). Revelation 13:12 repeats that his "deadly wound was healed." Later in the chapter, John elaborates about the "beast, which had the wound by a sword, and did live" (verse 14).

After Satan raises the Antichrist from the

dead, the Antichrist's partner, the False Prophet, will use this incredible event — probably watched by billions on the Internet, CNN, and other media outlets — to convince the world that the Antichrist is the long-awaited messiah. Once the Antichrist consolidates his control of Jerusalem and the Middle East, the False Prophet will force the people living under the jurisdiction of his world government to worship the Antichrist as "god." The 666 mark of the beast will be globally enforced as a totalitarian police control system. Those who submit to worship the Antichrist as "god" will accept the 666 mark on their foreheads or right hands. The righteous ones who reject the 666 will not be able to buy or sell anything and will be forced to go underground to escape being beheaded by the forces of the Antichrist (Revelation 20:4).

From that point until the battle of Armageddon, 1,260 days later, the world will be convulsed with spiritual and physical warfare between the forces of the Antichrist and the Jews and Gentiles who resist them. The Temple will probably be the initial battleground as the righteous priests battle to the death against supporters of the Antichrist. Revelation 12:17 warns that "the dragon was wroth [enraged] with the woman [Is-

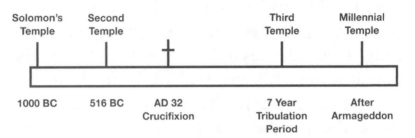

This time line shows the sequence of four temples in Jerusalem — two from history and two coming in the near future. Preparations are under way to build the Third Temple, and the Millennial Temple will be built by Jesus Christ when He returns.

rael; the people of Israel], and went to make war with the remnant of her seed, which keep the commandments of God, and have the testimony of Jesus Christ."

EZEKIEL'S VISION OF THE MILLENNIAL TEMPLE

One of the most hotly debated questions related to the future Temple is who will build it, the Jewish people or the coming Messiah? Some Jewish sages held that God's command in the Torah demands that Israel must first rebuild the Temple. Exodus 25:8 declares, "Let them make me a sanctuary;

that I may dwell among them." However, other authorities held that Israel should wait until the Messiah comes to build the Temple Himself. They pointed to the messianic message of the prophet Zechariah (6:12) where the prophet predicted: "Behold the man whose name is The BRANCH; and he shall grow up out of his place, and he shall build the temple of the LORD."

The resolution of this apparent contradiction will be found in the fact that the Scriptures declare there must be two more Temples in Israel's future. The Third Temple will be built by the Jews in the near future on the Temple Mount. This Third Temple is the one that will be defiled by the Antichrist, launching the Great Tribulation. Finally, the Third Temple will be cleansed by the coming of Jesus Christ as Israel's great High Priest and Messiah following His victory over the Antichrist in the battle of Armageddon. The Fourth Temple, described by the prophets Ezekiel and Zechariah, will then be built by Jesus the Messiah during the millennial kingdom, thus fulfilling both prophecies (see diagram). The Temple built by the Messiah will be the fourth and eternal Temple for the Millennium. This millennial Temple will exceed even the glory of the Third Temple.

The millennial Temple will be enormous, with walls extending more than one mile in each direction. In fact, the Fourth Temple will be so large that it could not possibly fit on the existing Temple Mount or even within the boundaries of the walled Old City of Jerusalem. The land measurements given in Ezekiel (chapters 40–48) indicate that the Messiah will build the Fourth Temple approximately twenty-five miles north of the walled city of Jerusalem.

In every detail this Fourth Temple differs from the Third Temple that must be built by the Jews on the present Temple Mount. The Scriptures do not say whether the Third Temple will coexist with the millennial Temple during the Millennium. However, in light of Daniel's prophecies that Christ will cleanse and sanctify the Third Temple after the Antichrist's defilement, it appears that the newly rebuilt Third Temple will continue to be used for worship during the thousand-year rule of Christ on earth. Israel will finally enjoy its long-awaited peace under the reign of the Messiah.

Additionally, Ezekiel prophesied a thirteenfold division of the land from Dan to Beer-sheba during the Millennium, which will provide each of Israel's twelve tribes with a parallel portion of land stretching horizontally from the Mediterranean Sea to the great Euphrates River (see Ezekiel 48:1–35). Each strip will be 25,000 rods in width measuring north to south (225,000 feet, or 43.25 miles wide). In the center of Israel a special portion of land called the Prince's Portion will be reserved for use by the Nassi, the Messiah (see Ezekiel 45:1–4). The Prince's Portion will contain the new, enlarged city of Jerusalem and the Fourth Temple. The dimensions of the new city of Jerusalem will be a 4,500-rod square, about 7.75 miles on each side.

Dr. Alfred Edersheim, the author of *The Temple,* explained that according to tradition, the boundary line between the ancient tribal allotment of Judah and Benjamin ran directly through the Old City of Jerusalem and the Temple.[5] Ezekiel describes the thirteenth portion of the land for the holy oblation (containing the millennial Temple, the new city of Jerusalem, and the Prince's Portion allotted to the Messiah) as lying between the tribal allotments of Judah and Benjamin once again (see Ezekiel 48:8–10, 22). While the other tribes will enjoy possession of their tribal portion forever, the prophet declares that the Levites will not inherit land. Instead, they will dwell in the portion known as the holy oblation with their beloved Messiah and receive their income from the Temple.

THE SIZE OF THE MILLENNIAL TEMPLE

The new Temple Mount area in the Millennium will be enormous. The Bible states, "There shall be for the sanctuary five hundred [rods] in length, with five hundred [rods] in breadth, square round about" (Ezekiel 45:2). A rod is equal to 6 cubits or 9 feet, when a cubit is defined as eighteen inches, so each side of the Fourth Temple will measure 4,500 feet — almost one mile long! The world has never seen such a massive structure. This measurement would yield a Temple area of 20.25 million square feet. For the sake of comparison, the Second Temple, built and enlarged by King Herod, was the largest Temple enclosure in history: it encompassed almost thirty-five acres. The entire Temple Mount area that survives today remains thirty-five acres. In other words, Ezekiel's prophecy revealed that the future millennial Temple will be *thirty-six times larger* than the Second Temple!

The glory of this millennial Temple will be manifested in the eternal presence of the Shekinah Glory of God. Ezekiel had witnessed in his earlier vision (see Ezekiel 11:22–23) the tragic departure of the Shekinah Glory from Solomon's Temple because of Israel's spiritual rebellion. Fortunately, God's plan of redemption for Israel and the Gentiles includes His promise that Jesus the Messiah will return in His glory to inhabit the Temple of God. When the Divine Presence dwells once again in Jerusalem, the Jews will take their position as God's chosen people in their Promised Land. Through Israel, God will bless all the nations of the world. God's promise was given through Ezekiel: "Then will I sprinkle clean water upon you, and ye shall be clean: from all your filthiness, and from all your idols, will I cleanse you" (Ezekiel 36:25). The prophecies reveal that it will not be long until the Messiah will return to fulfill all that God has promised concerning the redemption of Israel.

THIS IS THE LAST GENERATION

Since 1948 a series of remarkable events have set the stage for Israel to fulfill the ancient dream of rebuilding the holy sanctuary. We can confidently await the coming again of Jesus Christ in our lifetime. Jesus warned His disciples that the rebirth of Israel, the budding of the fig tree, would be the major prophetic sign that He will return within the same generation. "When ye shall see all these things, know that it is near, even at the doors. Verily I say unto you, This generation shall not pass, till all these things be fulfilled" (Matthew 24:33–34).

The apostle Paul warned that God "now commandeth all men every where to repent: because he hath appointed a day, in the which he will judge the world in righteousness by that man whom he hath ordained; whereof he hath given assurance unto all men, in that he hath raised him from the dead" (Acts 17:30–31). Every one of us faces a personal appointment with God. The writer of the book of Hebrews made this clear: "It is appointed unto men once to die, but after this the judgment" (Hebrews 9:27).

When the Jews offered sacrifices at the Tabernacle and the Temple, they did so as prophetic symbols of the ultimate and effective sacrifice of the blood of Jesus, the Lamb of God. The ancient sacrifices that were made at the earthly sanctuary were necessary to remind people of the sinfulness of their unredeemed nature and of the necessity of the sacrifice of innocent blood to atone for sins. However, Temple sacrifices only temporarily covered the sin of the people. Ultimately, sin needed to be atoned for by the death of the one true and perfect sacrifice, Jesus Christ, slain once and for all time (see Hebrews 9:23–24, 28). Jesus shed His innocent blood to atone for the sins of all who will repent of their sins and ask God to forgive them. The Scriptures declare, "Without shedding of blood is no remission [of sin]" (Hebrews 9:22).

We all will stand face to face with Jesus Christ to give an account of what we have done regarding our personal relationship with Him. Every one of us has lived in spiritual rebellion throughout our lives. The apostle Paul wrote, "For all have sinned, and come short of the glory of God" (Romans 3:23). We have all walked away from God's presence and have become unfit to enter heaven. God's Word declares, "For the wages of sin is death; but the gift of God is eternal life through Jesus Christ our Lord" (Romans 6:23). The Scriptures declare that our sinful rebellion has alienated each of us from the holy presence of God.

Jesus asked His disciples a vital question: "Whom say ye that I am?" And Simon Peter answered, "Thou art the Christ, the Son of the living God" (Matthew 16:15–16). Every one of us must answer this question. Our answer to that question will determine our eternal destiny. If we refuse to answer, we have already rejected Christ's claims to be our Savior. According to God's Word, the decisions and personal choices we make in this life have eternal consequences.

The Scriptures affirm that at the final judgment every human will submit to the Lord. The apostle Paul wrote, "As I live, saith the Lord, every knee shall bow to me, and every tongue shall confess to God. So then every one of us shall give account of himself to God" (Romans 14:11–12). The question is, will you choose to repent of your sins now and willingly bend your knee? Or will you reject His offer of salvation and finally be forced to bow your knee before your final Judge as you are sent to an eternity outside the presence of God?

When Jesus was crucified, He paid the complete price for your sins and mine. As the sinless Lamb of God, who personally deserved no punishment, Jesus allowed Himself to be offered as a perfect sacrifice for your sins, to reconcile you to the holiness of God. However, in a manner similar to a pardon offered to a prisoner awaiting execution, each of us must individually admit our guilt and repent of our sins and personally accept Christ's pardon. The basis of God's judgment following our death will be our personal relationship with Jesus Christ, not whether we were better or worse than most other people. Being a born-again Christian is not a matter of moral superiority or adherence to religion — it is a personal relationship with Jesus Christ.

Some people suggest that if God is truly a God of love, then He will bend the rules to allow "good" people into heaven, despite their rejection of Christ's gift of salvation. However, consider the real implications of this commonly held belief. If God allowed sinners who refused to repent of their sins to enter heaven, He would have to violate His nature as a holy and just God. Admitting unrepentant sinners into heaven would turn paradise into an annex of hell. If an unrepentant soul were allowed into heaven, that person's sinfulness would immediately destroy the holiness of heaven. In addition, an unrepentant sinner would naturally hate the holiness of heaven, its sinless inhabitants, and its continual worship of God. The sinless nature of a holy heaven and the evil nature of sin and unrepentant sinners make it impossible for God to forgive people's sins unless they sincerely repent.

When Nicodemus, one of the leaders of Israel's Sanhedrin Court, came to secretly visit Jesus at night, he asked Him about personal salvation. Jesus answered in the following words: "Verily, verily, I say unto thee, Except a man be born again, he cannot see the kingdom of God" (John 3:3). Becoming a Christian isn't a matter of intellectually accepting the facts about Christ and salvation. To be born again, you must repent of your sinful life, asking Christ to forgive you and placing your lifelong trust in Him as the Lord of your life. This decision will transform your life forever. The moment you commit your life to Christ, you receive God's promise of eternal life (see John 6:40). Though your body will die, you will live forever with Christ in heaven with a new, immortal body.

Jesus explained to Nicodemus, "For God so loved the world, that he gave his only begotten Son, that whosoever believeth in him should not perish, but have everlasting life. . . . He that believeth on him is not condemned: but he that believeth not is condemned already, because he hath not believed in the name of the only begotten Son of God" (John 3:16, 18).

The astonishing truth, difficult for many to believe, is that you merely have to accept Jesus Christ as your personal Savior and turn from your life of sin and pride in true repentance. Accept Him as your Lord and

Savior. The apostle John wrote, "But as many as received him, to them gave he power to become the sons of God, even to them that believe on his name" (John 1:12). The decision to accept Christ as your Savior is the most important decision you will ever make. Your choice will change your eternal destiny, and it will give you peace today as your guilt from a life of sin is removed forever.

All who have accepted Christ are called to be witnesses of Christ's message to the world. Our belief in the imminent Second Coming of Christ should motivate us to a renewed love of Christ and an eagerness to witness to unsaved friends and family. This belief we have in the Second Coming should motivate us to purify our daily walk before the Lord. As the apostle John wrote, "And every man that hath this hope in him purifieth himself, even as he is pure" (1 John 3:3). If you are a Christian, I challenge you to share the prophetic evidence in this book to witness to your friends and family about your faith in Jesus Christ.

As the prophetic clock ticks down toward the final midnight hour, the invitation of Christ is still open: "Behold, I stand at the door, and knock: if any man hear my voice, and open the door, I will come in to him,

and will sup with him, and he with me"
(Revelation 3:20).

POSSIBLE SEQUENCE OF KEY PROPHETIC EVENTS

1948	Rebirth of Israel.
1967	Israel captures Old City of Jerusalem and the Temple Mount.
1973	Yom Kippur War: Israel survives invasion from Syria, Egypt, Jordan, Iraq.
1980+	The Temple Institute researches and begins creation of vessels for Temple worship.

| 2005 | The Sanhedrin is reconvened for the first time since AD 425. The Temple location is determined by the Sanhedrin. Priests are trained in Temple sacrifice. |

ANTICIPATED PROPHETIC EVENTS

?	The Russian-Islamic alliance will attack Israel but will be defeated supernaturally.
?	Israel will build the Third Temple and resume the ancient Temple worship.
?	The ten nations (see Daniel 2:40–45) in Europe and surrounding Mediterranean nations will unite, forming the revived Roman Empire.

? A world dictator, the Antichrist, will rise to power over the revived Roman Empire and extend his global rule through military victories and peace treaties.

? The Antichrist will sign a seven-year security treaty with Israel (see Daniel 9:24–27).

? Halfway through the seven years, the Antichrist will stop the daily Temple sacrifice (see Daniel 12:11). The Antichrist will violate the Holy of Holies of the Third Temple.

?	Someone will assassinate the Antichrist; then he will rise from the dead and claim to be god, demanding worship as such. He will introduce the Mark of the Beast system.
?	The Antichrist's forces will attack righteous Jews and Gentiles who refuse to worship him.
?	Nations from Asia ("kings of the east") will lead a revolt against the Antichrist, raising a 200 million troop army and crossing Asia to engage in a massive military confrontation with the western military forces of the Antichrist.

?	The battle of Armageddon will occur seven years after the Antichrist signs the treaty with Israel.
?	Jesus Christ will defeat both armies to save Israel. He will enter through the sealed Eastern Gate of the Temple Mount into the rebuilt Temple. He will cleanse the sanctuary.

? Christ will establish His millennial kingdom from the throne of David in Jerusalem. Gentile nations will send representatives to the Temple to acknowledge their eternal allegiance to Christ (see Zechariah 14:16).

NOTES

INTRODUCTION: REBUILDING THE TEMPLE

1. J. T. Barclay, *The City of the Great King* (London: J. B. Lippincott, 1858), 9.
2. Moses Maimonides, *Mishneh Torah: Hilchos Bais HaBechirah* [The Laws of God's Chosen House], trans. and ed. Eliyahu Touger (Jerusalem: Maznaim Publishing, 1986), Introduction.

CHAPTER 1: PREPARING THE WAY FOR THE THIRD TEMPLE

1. Lactantius, *The Ante-Nicene Fathers,* vol. 7, *The Divine Institutes,* ed. Alexander Roberts (Grand Rapids: Eerdmans, 1988), 214.
2. Victorinus, *The Ante-Nicene Fathers,* vol. 7, *Commentary on the Apocalypse,* ed. Alexander Roberts (Grand Rapids: Eerdmans, 1988), 357.
3. Irenaeus, *The Ante-Nicene Fathers,* vol. 1,

Against Heresies, ed. Alexander Roberts (Grand Rapids: Eerdmans, 1988), 553.

4. Irenaeus, *Against Heresies,* 544.

5. Moses Maimonides, *Mishneh Torah: Hilchos Bais HaBechirah* [The Laws of God's Chosen House], trans. and ed. Eliyahu Touger (Jerusalem: Maznaim Publishing, 1986), 78.

6. "One Step in Heaven," a report on *60 Minutes,* broadcast on the CBS Television Network in March 1985.

7. This is the question that was asked in the poll: "The Temple Mount and Land of Israel Faithful Movement, headed by Gershon Salomon, put forth its main ideology on the struggle for Israeli sovereignty and the Jewish future of the Temple Mount, Jerusalem, and the land of Israel, and the rebuilding of the Temple. How likely would you be to support the idea of this movement?" Quoted in Randall Price, "Time for a Temple? Jewish Plans to Rebuild the Temple," *Israel My Glory,* January 1998, www.apocalypsesoon.org/xfile-4.html.

CHAPTER 2: THE GLORY OF JERUSALEM'S TEMPLE

1. David had set his heart on building a proper Temple to house the ark of the covenant and to provide a permanent place for offering sacrifices to God. His dream was reflected in his words to the prophet Nathan: "Lo, I dwell in an house of cedars, but the ark of the covenant of the LORD remaineth under curtains" (1 Chronicles 17:1).

2. Flavius Josephus, *Antiquities of the Jews* in *Josephus: Complete Works,* trans. William Whiston (Grand Rapids: Kregel, 1974), 174.

3. Louis Ginzberg, *The Legends of the Jews* (Philadelphia: Jewish Publication Society of America, 1968), 4:155.

4. The value of silver as of this writing is $13.50 per ounce, according to the World Silver Survey. "World Silver Survey 2007," GFMS, www.gfms.co.uk/publications_Silver_Survey.htm.

5. Josephus, *Antiquities of the Jews,* 175.

6. For more on this, see Alfred Edersheim, *The Temple* (New York: Hodder & Stoughton, 1904), 44.

7. For more on this, see Edersheim, *The Temple,* 45.

8. See Edersheim, *The Temple,* 47–49.

9. For more on this, see Richard F. Burton, *Personal Narrative of a Pilgrimage to Al-Madinah and Meccah* (London: G. Bell and Sons, 1913).

10. See Edersheim, *The Temple,* 35.

11. Flavius Josephus, *Wars of the Jews* in *Josephus: Complete Works,* trans. William Whiston (Grand Rapids: Kregel, 1974), 452.

12. W. Shaw Caldecott, *Herod's Temple: Its New Testament Associations and Its Actual Structure* (London: Charles H. Kelly, 1913), 41.

13. Tacitus, *The Histories by Publius Cornelius Tacitus,* trans. Alfred John Church and William Jackson Brodribb, book 5.12, http://mcadams.posc.mu.edu/txt/ah/tacitus/TacitusHistory05.html.

CHAPTER 3: RECOVERING LOST TEMPLE TREASURES

1. Bargil Pixner, "Unravelling the Copper Scroll Code: A Study on the Topography of 3Q15," *Revue de Qumran* 11, no. 43 (December 1983): 356.

2. Cited in Alfred J. Church, *The Story of the Last Days of Jerusalem from Josephus* (London: Seeley and Co., 1902), Preface.

3. Flavius Josephus, *Antiquities of the Jews* in *Josephus: Complete Works,* trans. William Whiston (Grand Rapids: Kregel, 1974), 294.

4. John Marco Allegro, *The Treasure of the Copper Scroll: The Opening and Decipherment of the Most Mysterious of the Dead Sea Scrolls: A Unique Inventory of Buried Treasure* (London: Routledge & Kegan Paul, 1960), 43, 149. See also Pixner, "Unravelling," 356.

5. See the Talmudic reference in Megillah, 26b.

6. Louis Ginzberg, *The Legends of the Jews* (Philadelphia: Jewish Publication Society of America, 1968), 4:325–26.

7. For readers who are interested in discovering more about these fascinating tablets, I would refer you to my book *Heaven: Homeward Bound* (WaterBrook Press, 1996).

8. J. T. Milik, "The Copper Scroll," *Revue Biblique* 1959, no. 66:567–75.

9. See Milik, "The Copper Scroll," 567–75.

CHAPTER 4: EXPLORING THE ANCIENT CITY UNDERNEATH JERUSALEM

1. See Alfred Edersheim, *The Temple* (New York: Hodder & Stoughton, 1904), 38.

2. Eliezer Azikri, *Sefer Charedim* [The Book of the Pious] (Venice, Italy, 1601).

3. Moses Maimonides, *Mishneh Torah: Hilchos Bais HaBechirah* [The Laws of God's Chosen House], trans. and ed. Eliyahu Touger (Jerusalem: Maznaim Publishing, 1986), 108.

4. See Edersheim, *The Temple,* 40.

5. Maimonides, *Mishneh Torah,* 198.

6. My own explorations of the underground city have been aided immeasurably by studying the notes of a series of adventurous 1800s Christian explorers, including Charles Wilson, Charles Warren, Eremete Pierotti, W. H. Barclay, and Edward Robinson.

7. Middoth 1.6 in *The Mishneh,* trans. Herbert Danby (New York: Oxford University Press, 1983), 591.

8. *Talmud,* Yoma 35a, ed., Leo Jung (London: Soncino Press, 1938), 161.

9. Shekalim 6.1 in *The Mishneh,* trans. Herbert Danby (Oxford, England: Oxford University Press, 1983), 158.

10. Maimonides, *Mishneh Torah,* 78.

11. Shekalim, 6.1 in *The Mishneh,* trans. Danby, 158.

12. Flavius Josephus described Herod's escape tunnel as follows: "There was also an occult [hidden] passage built for the

king; it led from Antonia to the inner temple, at its eastern gate; over which he also erected for himself a tower, that he might have the opportunity of a subterraneous ascent to the temple, in order to guard against any sedition which might be made by the people against their kings." (Flavius Josephus, *Antiquities of the Jews* in *Josephus: Complete Works,* trans. William Whiston [Grand Rapids: Kregel, 1974], 336.)

CHAPTER 5: THE THIRD TEMPLE IN THE LAST DAYS

1. Israel Eldad, "Should the Temple Be Rebuilt?" *Time,* June 30, 1967, www.time.com/time/archive/preview/0,10987,837052,00.html.
2. Moses Maimonides, *Mishneh Torah: Hilchos Bais HaBechirah* [The Laws of God's Chosen House], trans. and ed. Eliyahu Touger (Jerusalem: Maznaim Publishing, 1986), Introduction, 1.
3. Maimonides, *Mishneh Torah,* Translator's Introduction.
4. Israel Eldad, quoted in Randall Price, *The Coming Last Days' Temple* (Eugene, OR: Harvest House, 1999), 24.
5. See James Fleming, "The Undiscovered

Gate Beneath Jerusalem's Golden Gate," *Biblical Archeological Review,* January/February 1983, 24–37.

6. Eldad, "Should the Temple Be Rebuilt?"

7. The Jewish-Christian document *The Apocalypse of Peter* is dated AD 110.

CHAPTER 6: PRACTICAL PREPARATIONS FOR REBUILDING THE TEMPLE

1. "Sanhedrin Launched in Tiberias," IsraelNationalNews.com, January 20, 2005, www.israelnationalnews.com/news.php3?id=70349.

2. "Sanhedrin Launched in Tiberias."

3. Yaakov Katz, "Hear Ye, Hear Ye: Sanhedrin Seeks David's Scion as King," *Jerusalem Post,* January 12, 2005, www.call2christ.org/SanhedrinPage.html.

4. See Irvin Baxter Jr., "Sanhedrin Reborn After 1600 Years," *Endtime Magazine,* March/April 2005, 14.

5. For more on related developments, see "New 'Sanhedrin' Plans Rebuilding of Temple," WorldNetDaily.com, June 8, 2005, www.worldnetdaily.com/news/article.asp?ARTICLE_ID=44672.

6. "New 'Sanhedrin' Plans Rebuilding of Temple."

7. "New 'Sanhedrin' Plans Rebuilding of

Temple."

8. "Reestablished Sanhedrin Convenes to Discuss Temple," Israel NationalNews-.com, March 30, 2007, www.israelnational news.com/News/News.aspx/76624.

9. Moses Maimonides, "Letter on Religious Persecution," *The Guide of the Perplexed,* trans. Chaim Rabbin (London: Kegan Paul, 2006).

10. *Jerusalem Talmud,* ed. Heinrich W. Guggenheimer, Ma'aser Sheni 29 (New York: Walter de Gruyte, 2005).

11. *Babylonian Talmud,* Kerithoth 6b. See Leo Auerbach, *The Babylonian Talmud in Selection* (New York: Philosophical Library, 1944).

12. See Isaac Herzog, *The Royal Purple and the Biblical Blue: Argaman and Tekhelet: The Study of Chief Rabbi Dr. Isaac Herzog on the Dye Industries in Ancient Israel and Recent Scientific Contributions* (Jerusalem: Keter Publishing, 1989).

13. Richard N. Ostling, "Time for a New Temple?" *Time,* October 16, 1989, 65.

14. See Jeremy Shere, "A Very Holy Cow," *Jerusalem Post,* May 26, 1997, www.jpost .com/com/Archive/26.May.1997/Features/ Article-0.html.

15. *Sefer HaChinuch,* mitzvah 397, www .shemayisrael.com/parsha/kollel/archives/

chukas62.htm.

16. S. I. McMillen, *None of These Diseases* (Grand Rapids: Revell, 1984), 26.
17. *The Ante-Nicene Fathers,* vol. 1, *The Epistle of Barnabas,* ed. Alexander Roberts (Grand Rapids: Eerdmans, 1988), 142.

CHAPTER 7: NEW VESSELS FOR TEMPLE WORSHIP

1. In addition, Jews whose surname is Levi or a variation of Cohanim (such as the name Cohen) are considered descendants of the priestly lineage.
2. Bargil Pixner, "Unravelling the Copper Scroll Code: A Study on the Topography of 3Q15," *Revue de Qumran* 11, no. 43 (December 1983): 343.

CHAPTER 8: THE ARK OF THE COVENANT AND THE THIRD TEMPLE

1. See Arthur Bloomfield, *Where Is the Ark of the Covenant?* (Minneapolis: Bethany, 1976), 73–76.
2. Leo Roberts, "Travelling in the Highlands of Ethiopia," *National Geographic,* September 1935, 297.
3. "Aksum," *Encyclopaedia Britannica,* 2007 Encyclopaedia Britannica Online, www.britannica.com/eb/article-9005306/

Aksum.

4. From *B'nai B'rith Messenger,* January 1935, quoted in Bloomfield, *Where Is the Ark of the Covenant?* 39.

5. *Toronto Star,* July 19, 1981.

Chapter 9: Preparing for the Coming Messiah

1. The Balfour Declaration, http://domino .un.org/UNISPAL.NSF/fd807e46661e3 689852570d00069e918/e210ca73e38d9e 1d052565fa00705c61!Open Document.

2. "The Weizmann-Faisal Agreement," The Jewish Virtual Library, www.jewishvirtual library.org/jsource/History/faisaltext.html.

3. Emir Feisal, "Letter to Felix Frankfurter," March 3, 1919, www.amislam.com/ feisal.htm.

4. Sources for the value of minerals harvested from the Dead Sea: Harry Rimmer, *The Shadow of Coming Events* (Grand Rapids: Eerdmans, 1950), 4. Potassium chloride, $85 per short ton (2000 lbs.), www.the-innovation-group.com/Chem Profiles/Potash.htm. Magnesium bromide, $0.0.64 per pound, list, bulk, tl., works, www.the-innovation-group.com/Chem Profiles/Bromine.htm.

5. See Alfred Edersheim, *The Temple* (New

York: Hodder & Stoughton, 1904), 38–39.

SELECT BIBLIOGRAPHY

Allegro, John Marco. *The Treasure of the Copper Scroll: The Opening and Decipherment of the Most Mysterious of the Dead Sea Scrolls, a Unique Inventory of Buried Treasure.* London: Routledge & Kegan Paul, 1960.

Auerbach, Leo. *The Babylonian Talmud in Selection.* New York: Philosophical Library, 1944.

Barclay, J. T. *The City of the Great King, or, Jerusalem as It Was, as It Is, and as It Is to Be.* London: J. B. Lippincott, 1858.

Ben-Dov, Meir. *In the Shadow of the Temple: The Discovery of Ancient Jerusalem.* New York: Harper & Row, 1985.

Berman, Joshua. *The Temple: Its Symbolism and Meaning Then and Now.* London: Jason Aronson, 1995.

Besant, Walter, and E. H. Palmer. *Jerusalem, The City of Herod and Saladin.* London: Chatto & Windus, 1908.

Bloomfield, Arthur. *Where Is the Ark of the Covenant?* Minneapolis: Bethany, 1976.

Caldecott, W. Shaw. *Herod's Temple: Its New Testament Associations and Its Actual Structure.* London: Charles H. Kelly, 1913.

Church, Alfred J. *The Story of the Last Days of Jerusalem from Josephus.* London: Seeley and Co., 1902.

Conner, Kevin J. *The Temple of Solomon.* Portland, OR: BT Publishing, 1988.

Edersheim, Alfred. *Bible History, Old Testament.* Grand Rapids: Eerdmans, 1982.

————. *The Life and Times of Jesus the Messiah.* 2 vols. New York: Longman, Brown, Green, and Longmans, 1896.

————. *The Temple.* New York: Hodder & Stoughton, 1904.

Eisemann, Moshe. *Ezekiel: A New Commentary Anthologized from Talmudic, Midrashic and Rabbinical Sources.* Brooklyn, NY: Mesorah Publications, 1980.

Fergusson, James. *The Temples of the Jews and the Other Buildings in the Haram Area at Jerusalem.* London: John Murray, 1878.

Freeman, Hobart E. *An Introduction to the Old Testament Prophets.* Chicago: Moody Press, 1968.

Goldwurm, Hersh. *Daniel: A New Transla-*

tion with a Commentary Anthologized from Talmudic, Midrashic and Rabbinical Sources. Brooklyn, NY: Mesorah Publications, 1980.

Ice, Thomas, and Randall Price. *Ready to Rebuild: The Imminent Plan to Rebuild the Last Days Temple.* Eugene, OR: Harvest House, 1992.

Josephus, Flavius. *Antiquities of the Jews* in *Josephus: Complete Works.* Translated by William Whiston. Grand Rapids: Kregel Publications, 1974.

————— . *Wars of the Jews* in *Josephus: Complete Works.* Translated by William Whiston. Grand Rapids: Kregel Publications, 1974.

Kellogg, Samuel H. *The Jews; or, Prediction and Fulfillment: An Argument for the Times.* New York: A. D. F. Randolph & Co., 1883.

Lewin, Thomas. *Jerusalem: A Sketch of the City and Temple from the Earliest Times to the Siege by Titus.* London: Longman, Green, Longman, and Roberts. 1861.

Lewis, T. Hayter. *The Holy Places of Jerusalem.* London: John Murray, 1888.

Ludwigson, R. *A Survey of Bible Prophecy.* Grand Rapids: Zondervan, 1951.

Maimonides, Moses. *Mishneh Torah: Hilchos Bais HaBechirah* [The Laws of God's

Chosen House]. Translated and edited by Eliyahu Touger. Jerusalem: Maznaim Publishing, 1986.

McCall, Thomas S., and Zola Levitt. *Satan in the Sanctuary.* Chicago: Moody Press, 1974.

Parrott, Andre. *The Temple of Jerusalem.* New York: Philosophical Library, 1955.

Pixner, Bargil. "Unravelling the Copper Scroll Code: A Study on the Topography of 3Q15." *Revue de Qumran* 11, no. 43 (December 1983): 323–66.

Reynolds, James, trans. *The History of the Temple of Jerusalem: Translated from the Arabic Manuscript, with Notes and Dissertations.* London: A. J. Valpy, 1836.

Reznick, Leibel. *The Holy Temple Revisited.* London: Jason Aronson, 1990.

Richman, Chaim. *The Light of the Temple: Art, History, Service.* Jerusalem: The Temple Institute, 1998.

Ritmeyer, Leen. *The Quest: Revealing the Temple Mount in Jerusalem.* Jerusalem: Lamb Foundation, 2006.

Roberts, Alexander, ed. *The Ante-Nicene Fathers.* 10 vols. Grand Rapids: W. B. Eerdmans, 1988.

Rosenau, Helen. *Vision of the Temple: The Image of the Temple of Jerusalem in Juda-*

ism and Christianity. London: Oresko Books, 1979.

Schaffer, Shaul, with Asher Joseph. The Divine Dwelling. Brooklyn, NY: Unknown, 1975.

Schmitt, John W., and J. Carl Laney. Messiah's Coming Temple: Ezekiel's Prophetic Vision of the Future Temple. Grand Rapids: Kregel, 1997.

Steinberg, Shalom Dov. The Mishkan and the Holy Garments. Jerusalem: Toras Chaim Institute, 1992.

————— . The Third Beis HaMikdash [The Third Temple]. Jerusalem: Moznaim Publications, 1993.

Stewart, Don, and Chuck Missler. The Coming Temple. Orange, CA: Dart Press, 1991.

Thrupp, Joseph Francis. Ancient Jerusalem: A New Investigation into the History, Topography and Plan of the City, Environs, and Temple: Designed Principally to Illustrate the Records and Prophecies of Scripture. Cambridge, England: Macmillan, 1855.

Williams, George. The Holy City: Historical, Topographical, and Antiquarian Notices of Jerusalem. London: John W. Parker, 1849.

Wilson, Charles, and Charles Warren. The Recovery of Jerusalem: A Narrative of Exploration and Discovery in the City and *the Holy Land.* London: Richard Bentley, 1871.

ABOUT THE AUTHOR

Grant R. Jeffrey is the wauthor of nearly twenty-five books, including *The Next World War, Surveillance Society, Armageddon, The Signature of God,* and *Prince of Darkness.* He also is the editor of the *Marked Reference Prophecy Study Bible.* His decades of study in the areas of prophecy, history, theology, and archaeology are reflected in his latest book, *The New Temple and the Second Coming.* Jeffrey's dozens of research trips to the Middle East and his extensive interviews with religious and political leaders in Israel provide the background to the insights found in this book.

His books have been translated into twenty-four languages and have sold more than seven million copies throughout the world. His popular television program, *Bible Prophecy Revealed,* is broadcast twice weekly on Trinity Broadcasting Network.

He also appears frequently as a guest on television and radio.

Jeffrey's passion for research has led him to acquire a personal library of more than seven thousand books on prophecy, theology, and biblical archaeology. He earned his master's degree and a Doctor of Philosophy in Biblical Studies from Louisiana Baptist University. Before becoming a full-time writer, he was a professional financial planner for eighteen years with his own brokerage company in western Canada.